Testimonies/Endorsements

ᴖ

God's Word is timeless, and Joe & Ruth Wesley offer a well organized access to meditate upon the richness of the Bible. This is a helpful book for all who long to drink deeply from the Scriptures!
Reverend Andrew P. Ricci
Pastor, St. Francis de Sales
Spooner, Wisconsin

For the committed Christian seeking challenging insights into ordinary experiences, this book is a compelling guide for growing in faith. Through concrete personal experiences and their scriptural connections, we are led to a deeper union with Jesus Christ while addressing the demanding issues of daily life.
Sister Richelle Ranallo, O.S.F.
Pastoral Minister, Parishes of:
St. Joseph's, Shell Lake, WI;
St Catherine's, Sarona, WI;
St. Francis de Sales, Spooner, WI.

One of the greatest blessings I enjoy in my private time is when I pray through Scripture. During these moments I pray that Scripture which is before me. Praying God's Promises *provides not only the opportunity of praying through Scripture but also acts as a type of prayer manual offering quick links to a subject that may be most pressing at the time.*

For those who already know the rich blessing of praying through Scripture or for someone experiencing it for the first time, I highly recommend Joe and Ruth Wesley's Praying God's Promises.
Reverend Kevin L. Norton
Pastor, Christian and Missionary Alliance Church
Hibbing, Minnesota

PRAYING GOD'S PROMISES

Proverbs 4:20-22
My son, attend to my words, incline your ear unto my sayings. Let them not depart from thine eyes; keep them in the midst of thine heart. For they are life unto those that find them, and health to all their flesh.

PRAYING GOD'S PROMISES

by
Joseph and Ruth
Wesley

Peace and God's Blessing

Joe & Ruth

A Life Changing Book Published by
River City Press

PRAYING GOD'S PROMISES

Copyright 2003, Joseph & Ruth Wesley
of Spooner, WI. All rights reserved.

No part of this book may be reproduced in any manner without the written permission of the publisher. Brief quotations may be used by Pastors, Teachers, and Reviewers for use in magazines, newspapers, or on broadcasts, when the source of material is acknowledged.

Scripture references from the Old Testament are used from the Authorized King James Bible.

Scripture references from the New Testament are taken from the Revised Standard Version (RSV) published by Augsburg Fortress. Copyright 1946, 1952 and 1971 by the Division of Christian Education of the National Council of the Churches of Christ in the USA. Used with permission. Also, New American Standard (NASB), Copyright: 1960, 1962, 1963, 1968, 1971, 1972, 1973, 1975, 1977 and 1995, by the Lockman Foundation. Used with permission.

ISBN No. 0-9706962-5-6

Cover Design & Graphics
Dianne & Chris Holland Tuve

Edited by: LaVerne B. Lein

Published by:
River City Press
http://www.rivercitypress.net
4301 Emerson Avenue N.
Minneapolis, MN 55412

Dedication

We dedicate this book to our children, Tom, Jean and Frank. You have lived with, and through, this journey of faith with us. While the journey has never been easy, it certainly has been interesting, and you have always been a part of it.

You are treasures we hold in our hearts. We love you!

Acknowledgement

As with anything that we do, we never do it alone. There are several people who walked with us on this journey of faith. We gratefully say, "Thank you," to each one of you.

A very special "Thank You" to Reverend Ray Anderson for having such an interest in this book and who made the first phone call to our publisher.

Thanks to: our publisher, Bob Wolf, for his help and encouragement in getting our book published.

Evangelist Bill Maginnis whose love and prayers, workshops, teachings, tapes and Scripture studies launched us into our relationship with Jesus and taught us both so much about who we are in Christ.

Bill's wife Kathy who is the prayer force behind Bill, and his daughter Julie who reinforced her dad's teaching and taught so much herself.

Lenore Sypnieski, who is a beautiful servant of God that loved us unconditionally enough to pray for and with, talk to, scold, cry with and encourage us so much as we started our faith journey and continues today. May her jewels be bright and her mansion big enough for all the "kids." Lord. Thank you, we love you.

Evangelist Ed and Colleen Klein, our friends from Portland, Oregon, who raised up Bill Maginnis in his ministry. They have Living Water Ministry and Ed Klein Evangelistic Association. They are beautiful examples of trusting the Lord and awesome teachers of God's Word. Our lives are much richer because of you.

Deacon Bill Warren, Deacon Bill Brennan, Father Bill Adams, and Father James Nisbet who have a way of opening up the Scriptures and helped us see Jesus.

Our San Andreas bunch. These dear SAINTS who knew us "when" and know us now and who still love us! Their love of Jesus would break out into songs of praise and thanksgiving and prayers for whatever was needed for any one of us. Dr. Duane and Barbara Verhalen (Barbara is Joe's prayer partner), Joe and Rose Rodelo, Ken and Remy Hamann, Robert and Elizabeth Jenkins, Carl and Judy Eschen, Barbara Craddock, Leigh Ann Roberts, Sylvia Varain, (Ruth's prayer partner), Suzanne Gruna, Frank and Linda Kripal, Frances Gardner, Frank and Pam Muschalek, John and Ronnie Pargett, Dick and Donna Davis, and Deacon Bob and Millie Rego.

Each of them showed us so much of the love of Jesus in countless ways and taught us to love unconditionally.

We especially say, "Thank You" to our Pastor, Reverend Andrew Ricci. We will be forever grateful for his encouragement on this end of our journey.

Contents

Part One
Jesus Christ of Nazareth
The Way, The Truth, and The Life

You Are Loved	2
The Endless Fruitless Search	2
One Man's Love	3
Absolute Love	3
Yours for The Asking	4
Prayer of Commitment	4
The Blood of Jesus - What It Gives Freely	5
Redemption, Justification, Righteousness	6
Sanctification	7
Remission	7
Reconciled	8
Overcoming Power	8
Delivered, Forgiveness	8
Boldness	9
Business Problems	10
Baptism of The Holy Spirit	11
Salvation and Baptism of the Holy Spirit	13
Believing vs. Unbelief - Benedictions	15
Receive God's Righteousness with The Prayer of Faith	15
Our Unchanging God	16
Our Story of Praying God's Promises	20
What About Prayer?	21
Praise	22
Shouts of Joy Bring Us Out of Bondage	23

Part Two
Faith in Action
Testimonies of God's Love,
Faithfulness, and Awesome Power

Healing of A Unstable Heart	26
Panic, Prayer and Praise	27
God Divides the Flames of the Old Gulch Fire	29
God Works Through His People	32
God Is the Provision for His People	32

Part Three
Take God at His Word

God's Promises 36
Hindrances Blocking Prayer 38

Prayer Alphabet

Absentmindedness 48
Afflictions 48
Anger 49
Anxiety 49
Asking God 50
Binding and Loosing 51
Child Training 53
Comfort in Disappointments 54
Comfort for Mourners 55
Condemnation 55
Confession/Reconciliation 56
Confidence 58
Confusion 60
Counseling 60
Death 61
Deliverance from Addiction 62
Depression 66
Discouragement and Disappointments 66
Faith-Wavering 69
Families for a Closer Walk 71
Families-Praying for Our Children 71
Families-Children in False Religion 73
Farmers Provision 74
Fasting 75
Fear 78
Meditations 79
Fear of Man 81
Fear of The Lord 81
Forgiveness 84
God's Presence 86
Guidance and Direction 87
Healing Scriptures for All Needs 89-110
Heartache 110
Intercession 111

Judgment	112
Judging The Gift of Prophecy	113
Judging Prophets	114
Kingdom of God	115
Keys to The Kingdom of God	115
Laying on of Hands for Blessing	116
Learning	118
Lost articles and people	119
Love of Brethren	119
Love and Care of The Father	121
Maintaining Deliverance	123
Marriages	124
Oppression	127
Overcoming The Powers of Darkness	127
Patience	128
Peace	130
Pharmakeia-Sorcery, etc.	130
Poverty	132
Praise and Thanks	133
Prayer	135
Pride	137
Prosperity	137
Protection	138
Rebellion	140
Righteousness	142
Salvation	143
Shield of Faith	150
Sin	153
Strength	155
Temptation	156
Tithing	157
Tribulation	158
Trust	159
Voice-Testing	160
When The Lord Speaks to Us	162
When The Devil Speaks to Us	164
When Our Flesh Gets in The Way	165
Visions	166
Weight Control	167
Will of God	170
Wisdom	171
Word	173

Part One

☙

*Jesus Christ of Nazareth
The Way, The Truth
and The Life*

"There is salvation in no one else
for there is no other name
under heaven
that has been given
among men by which
we must be saved."
Acts 4:12

Our dear friend Lenore Sypnieski gave us this "You Are Loved" letter at the start of our conversion. Thank you, Lenore. We shall be forever grateful!

You Are Loved

Way down deep inside, it is love we really want more than anything else in the world, isn't it?

Not wealth, fame, power, or pleasure, but someone to love us unconditionally—without reservation, and forever. We want someone who really cares, who knows us completely (our ideals and frustrations, our hopes and fears, our strengths and weaknesses—all the good and all the bad) and who loves us anyway.

We want someone who makes us feel complete and whole inside; someone who makes us feel worthy and special just by loving us; and someone whose love makes us strong, free, and more loving.

We tell ourselves that such love exists only in dreams and fairy tales, and that we must be realistic. We believe the desire—that need—is an immature, unhealthy thing. Yet, in spite of all that, buried somewhere beneath all our denial and suppression, remains our overwhelming need to be loved and accepted. Part of us never ceases to search for this love.

The Endless, Fruitless Search

We search for love in parents, friends, lovers, husbands, wives, and children. We even scan strange eyes at parties, or on subway trains, wondering and hoping . . . .

Sometimes, for a while, we think we have found it. For a couple of days, or weeks, or months, we think we've found that unbelievable thing – someone who truly loves us, who really cares about us, who wants only the best for us, even at their own expense.

But somehow, sooner or later, every single one of them ends up letting us down and disappointing us. They take advantage of us, or deceive us, or perhaps they just end up being "human" – a little selfish, a little unkind, and a little unreliable. And we disappoint them, too, if we're honest with ourselves.

It is a very curious thing, is it not? That all human beings – old women and men and new-born babies, Harvard graduates and aboriginal tribesmen, corporation presidents and beggars – all experience this need for love, and yet it is a need for which there is no apparent fulfillment.

For every other need we have, there exists something to fulfill it. We hunger, and there is bread. We thirst, and there is water. We need challenge, recognition, companionship, creative expression, and for all of these there are possibilities for fulfillment.

Is it logical then, that there should be no possibility for fulfillment of our need to be loved — perhaps the most powerful and universal of all our needs? Such love must exist somewhere! Perhaps we've just been looking in the wrong places, and for the wrong people.

One Man's Love

There was only one man who ever loved like that—completely, unconditionally, and without reservation—only one man, who was even willing to die for those He loved. And that love was not confined to His mother, or His friends, or a particular woman. He loved everyone like that.

He shocked people with that love. They didn't understand how He could love criminals, prostitutes, drunkards, and corrupt bureaucrats. They had never seen such powerful love. Nor had they seen such transforming love, for once it had touched people, they were never the same again. Once they knew they were loved, the prostitutes became godly women, the drunkards stopped drinking, and the bureaucrats returned their stolen money.

The religious people called Him a blasphemer. The self-righteous called Him a son of the devil. Others call Him insane.

However, His friends call Him . . . JESUS.

Absolute Love

Everything He did, everything He said, revealed an extraordinary man—a man who loved as no other man or woman has loved before or since.

When people were hungry, He fed them; and when they were sick, He healed them. When they were weak and fearful, He gave them strength and courage; and when they were discouraged, He gave them hope. When they mourned, He comforted them, and when the sin and death in their lives was too great to bear, He took their death on Himself and gave them His own eternal life.

You say that's all very well for those who lived with Him, but you ask, "What good does that do me? He died two thousand years ago!"

And that's the most extraordinary thing of all - because He isn't dead. He's ALIVE!

So He is not just a loving man, or a great moral teacher, or a dead prophet. He is the Son of the Living God, the resurrected Messiah, the Creator of all life, and the Giver of all love. He's alive! And He has promised to protect, strengthen, comfort and love you, forever.

One of His followers said that nothing would ever be able to separate you from that love: "Who will separate us from the love of Christ? I am convinced that neither death nor life, neither angels nor principalities, nor things present, nor things to come, nor powers, nor height, nor depth, nor any other created thing will be able to separate us from the love of God which is in Christ Jesus our Lord."

(Romans 8:38-39)

We experience the overwhelming need for love, because we are created to be loved by God, whose very nature is love.

Yours for the Asking

There is only one condition. God has always loved you. But in order to experience God's love personally, you must ask Him into your life and into your heart. He gave you a free will, and He will never violate it. He will never force Himself, or His love, upon you. The choice is yours, to invite Him in, or to shut Him out. There is no middle ground.

Some people think that inviting God in is a great risk, but it is only the risk of abandoning yourself to perfect love.

This love is a gift. There is nothing you can do to earn it. He does not ask you to give up anything, to clean up your life, or to get yourself together in order to receive it. He only wants to love you, and to let you know that there is only your own choice separating you from the life and love and joy and peace of God.

"For God so loved the world that He gave His one and only begotten Son, that whoever believes in Him shall not perish, but have eternal life." John 3:16

Prayer of Commitment

Open your heart to God with absolute trust and pray:

"Lord Jesus, I am sorry for my sins (name them to Him in prayer, and resolve to turn away from them – repent.) I have tried to turn away from them, but I need You, Jesus to be my Lord and Savior. Help me to let you be Lord in all areas of my life. I submit myself to Your will. I ask for Your Holy Spirit to be in my mind, on my lips and in my heart, to bring me closer in love

to You and everyone. *Thank You for taking the penalty for my sins. Thank You for saving me!*" (It's important to immediately tell someone publicly of your commitment to Jesus Christ.)

We challenge you to post this prayer, or one like it in your own words. Place it where you can see it every morning, and say it every day for 30 days. Your life will change!

THE BLOOD OF JESUS—This is what it gives to us freely

Salvation: An act of being born again; being saved from eternal damnation.

John 3: 3,5-7 Jesus answered and said to him, "Truly, truly, I say to you, unless one is born again he cannot see the kingdom of God."
Jesus answered, "Truly, truly, I say to you, unless one is born of the water and the Spirit he cannot enter into the kingdom of God. That which is born of the flesh is flesh; that which is born of the Spirit is spirit. "Do not be amazed that I said to you, 'You must be born again.'"

John 3:17 For God did not send the Son into the world to judge the world, but that the world might be saved through Him.

Acts 4:12 "And there is salvation in no one else; for there is no other name under heaven that has been given among men by which we must be saved."

Please see section on Salvation for further benefits.

Atonement: That which blots out, covers over, satisfies the sin debt of mankind.

Leviticus 17:11 For the life of the flesh is in the blood: and I have given it to you upon the altar to make an atonement for your souls: for it is the blood that makes an atonement for the soul.

Romans 5:10-11	For if while we were enemies we were reconciled to God through the death of His Son, much more, having been reconciled, we shall be saved by His life. And not only this, but we also exult in God through our Lord Jesus Christ, through whom we have now received the reconciliation.
Redemption:	The contract on our life is paid in full, bought back from the power of sin and death.
Psalms 107:1-2	O give thanks unto the LORD, for He is good; For His mercy endures forever. Let the redeemed of the LORD say so, whom He hath redeemed from the hand of the enemy.
Ephesians 1:7	In whom we have redemption through his blood, the forgiveness of our sins, according to the riches of his grace.
Revelation 5:9	And they sang a new song, saying, "Worthy are You to take the book and to break the seals; for You were slain, and purchased for God with Your blood men from every tribe and people and nation.
Justification:	We have been acquitted of guilt and sin.
Romans 5:9	Much more than, having been justified by His blood, we shall be saved from the wrath of God through Him.
Acts 13:38-39	"Therefore let it be known to you, brethren, that through Him forgiveness of sins is proclaimed to you, and through Him everyone who believes is freed from all things, from which you could not be freed through the Law of Moses.
Righteousness:	We have right-standing with God.
Romans 3:22-23	Even the righteousness of God through faith in Jesus Christ for all who believe. For there is no distinction; for all have sinned and fall short of the glory of God.

Romans 3:25-26	Whom God displayed publicly as a propitiation in His blood through faith. This was to demonstrate His righteousness, because in the forbearance of God He passed over the sins previously committed; for the demonstration, I say, of His righteousness at the present time, so that He would be just and the justifier of the one who has faith in Jesus.
Sanctification:	We are set apart to God, through the blood of Jesus.
I Corinthians 1:30	But by His doing are you in Christ Jesus, who became to us wisdom from God, and righteousness and sanctification, and redemption.
Hebrews 10:10	By this will we have been sanctified through the offering of the body of Jesus Christ once for all.
Hebrews 10:14	For by one offering He has perfected for all time those who are sanctified.
Luke 22:17-20	And when He had taken a cup and given thanks, He said, "Take this and share it among yourselves; for I say to you, I will not drink of the fruit of the vine from now on until the kingdom of God comes." And when He had taken some bread and given thanks, He broke it and gave it to them, saying, "This is My body which is given for you; do this in remembrance of Me." And in the same way He took the cup after they had eaten, saying, "This cup which is poured out for you is the new covenant in My blood."
Remission:	Sins' debt has been completely cancelled.
Romans 3:24	Being justified as a gift by His grace through the redemption which is in Christ Jesus.
Romans 3:25	Whom God displayed publicly as a propitiation in His blood through faith. This was to demonstrate

His righteousness, because in the forbearance of God He passed over the sins previously committed;

Reconciled: What we become after accepting Christ's redemption.

Colossians 1:20 And through Him to reconcile all things to Himself, having made peace through the blood of His cross; through Him I say, whether things on earth or things in heaven.

Romans 5:10 For if while we were enemies we were reconciled to God through the death of His Son, much more, having been reconciled, we shall be saved by His life.

Overcoming Power: We receive it as we appropriate what has been given to us.

Luke 10:19 "Behold, I have given you authority to tread on serpents and scorpions, and over all the power of the enemy, and nothing will injure you.

Revelation 12:11 And they over came him because of the blood of the Lamb and because of the word of their testimony, and they did not love their life even when faced with death.

Delivered: We are released from captivity and the powers of darkness.

II Corinthians 1:10 Who delivered us from so great a peril of death, and will deliver us, He on whom we have set our hope. And He will yet deliver us.

Colossians 1:13 For He rescued us from the dominion of darkness, and transferred us to the kingdom of His beloved Son.

Forgiveness: We have been pardoned and all transgressions forgotten.

Colossians 1:14 In whom we have redemption, the forgiveness of sins.

I John 1:9	If we confess our sins, He is faithful and righteous to forgive us our sins and to cleanse us from all unrighteousness.
Matthew 26:28	For this is My blood of the covenant, which is poured out for many for forgiveness of sins.
Boldness:	We come right to the throne-room of God.
Proverbs 28:1	The wicked flee when no man pursues: but the righteous are as bold as a lion.
Luke 21: 14-15	So make up your minds not to prepare beforehand to defend yourselves; for I will give you utterance and wisdom which none of your opponents will be able to resist or refute.
Ephesians 3:11-12	This was in accordance with the eternal purpose which He carried out in Christ Jesus our Lord, in whom we have boldness and confident access through faith in Him.
Ephesians 6:19	And pray on my behalf, that utterance may be given to me in the opening of my mouth, to make known with boldness the mystery of the gospel.
Philippians 1:20	According to my earnest expectation and hope, that I will not be put to shame in anything, but that with all boldness, Christ will even now, as always, be exalted in my body, whether by life or by death.
Hebrews 4:14-16	Therefore, since we have a great high priest who has passed through the heavens, Jesus the Son of God, let us hold fast our confession. For we do not have a high priest who cannot sympathize with our weaknesses, but One who has been tempted in all things, as we are, yet without sin.

Business Problems

Deuteronomy 31:6	Be strong and of a good courage, fear not, nor be afraid of them: for the LORD thy God, He it is that doth go with thee; He will not fail thee nor forsake thee.
Joshua 1:7	Only thou be strong and very courageous, that thou may observe to do according to all the law, which Moses my servant commanded thee: turn not from it to the right hand or to the left, that thou may prosper wherever thou goest.
Job 22:21	Acquaint thyself now with Him, and be at peace: thereby good shall come unto thee.
Jeremiah 32:27	Behold, I am the LORD, the God of all flesh: is there anything too hard for Me?
Psalms 35:27	Let them shout for joy, and be glad, that favor my righteous cause: yea, let them say continually, "Let the LORD be magnified, which hath pleasure in the prosperity of His servant"
Psalms 46:1	God is our refuge and strength, a very present help in trouble.
Psalms 55:18	He hath delivered my soul in peace from the battle that was against me: for there were many with me.
Psalms 55:22	Cast thy burden upon the LORD, and He will sustain thee: He shall never suffer the righteous to be moved.
Psalms 68:19	Blessed be the Lord, who daily loads us with benefits, even the God of our salvation.
Proverbs 3:5	Trust in the LORD with all thy heart; and lean not unto thine own understanding.

Proverbs 8:21	That I may cause those that love me to inherit substance; and I will fill their treasures.
Proverbs 16:3	Commit thy works unto the LORD, and thy thoughts shall be established.
Proverbs 23:26	My son give me thy heart, and let thine eyes observe my ways.
Proverbs 22:29	See thou a man diligent in his business? He shall stand before kings; he shall not stand before mean men.
Isaiah 41:13	For I the LORD will hold thy right hand, saying unto thee, Fear not; I will help thee.
Luke 6:38	"Give and it will be given unto you. They will pour into your lap a good measure - pressed down, shaken together, and running over. For by your standard of measure it will be measured to you in return."
Proverbs 19:17	He that hath pity upon the poor lends unto the LORD; and that which hath been given He will pay him again.
John 15:7	"If you abide in Me, and My words abide in you, ask whatever you wish, and it will be done for you."
Philippians 4:19	And my God will supply all your needs according to His riches in glory in Christ Jesus.
III John 2	Beloved, I pray that in all respects that you may prosper and be in good health, just as your soul prospers.

BAPTISM OF THE HOLY SPIRIT

Look up these scriptures. Ask God to reveal His truth.

1. Any and all involvement with the occult and their activities must be renounced.

2. You must be born again. — John 3:3-7

3. Prophecy of baptism — Isaiah 29:9-16
Joel 2:28

4. Tells of two baptisms — Matthew 3:11
Luke 3:16
Acts 8:14-17
Acts 1: 4-5
Acts 19:1-6

5. Jesus told us how to worship the Father this way.
John 4:23-24
John 7:37-39

6. Jesus said the Words that He has spoken are Spirit and Life to us.
John 6:63

7. Will our Father God give us something from the devil? (No, never).
Luke 11:9-13

8. Jesus said these signs should follow believers, not unbelievers.
Mark 16:17
1Cor. 14:22

9. Obey God, not men. — Acts 5:29
1 Cor. 14:39

10. Receive the promises spoken of in: — Acts 2:33, 39
Acts 1:4-5; 2:4; 10:46; 11:15; 19:6

11. At Pentecost, all 120 people including Mary, the Blessed Mother spoke in tongues. This gift is mentioned 57 times in the New Testament. — Acts 1:14
1 Cor. 14:2
Romans 8:26-27

12. Paul, converted on the road to Damascus called Jesus Lord. (1Corinthians 12:3) Ananias was sent 3 days later to lay hands on him to be filled with the Holy Spirit. Obviously, then Paul did not receive the evidence of Baptism of the Holy Spirit when he experienced salvation.

Acts 9:5-6
Romans 10:13
Romans 10:9-10

SALVATION AND THE BAPTISM OF THE HOLY SPIRIT

Use the following verses and put the name of each person for whom you are praying into each scripture, to receive the baptism of the Holy Spirit. You may also want to write the scriptures and read them out loud, as it helps you to open your heart to the Lord.

A. **Acts 16:31**
They said, "Believe in the Lord Jesus and you will be saved, you and your household."
Pray the Promise; Believe the Promise; Live and speak the Word to the members of your household.
God's word says this.

B. **Colossians 4:3**
Praying at the same time for us as well, that God will open up to us a door for the Word, so that we may speak forth the mystery of Christ Jesus, for which also I have been imprisoned.

C. **Matthew 5:6**
Blessed are those who hunger and thirst for righteousness, for they shall be satisfied.

Hunger and thirst. Jesus will give people the hunger and thirst for Him, and for spiritual things.

D. **John 6:44,**
No one can come to Me unless the Father who sent Me draws him, and I will raise him up on the last day.

John 14:6
Jesus said to him, "I am the way, and the truth, and the life; no one comes to the Father but through Me."
The Father will draw them to Himself. Only God can draw a person into submission by His Spirit (John 1:12-13).

E. **Psalm 37:3-5**
Trust in the LORD and do good; so shall thou dwell in the land, and verily thou shall be fed. Delight thyself also in the LORD; and he shall give thee the desires of thine heart. Commit thy way unto the LORD; trust also in him, and he shall bring it to pass.

What is faith? It is the confident assurance that what we hope for is going to happen. It is the evidence of things we cannot yet see.

Now you will see spiritual warfare, because Satan will try to come against this. He doesn't want to lose anyone, and he will encourage you to doubt that your prayers will be answered. Don't let Satan break your spirit! Verbalize God's promises to join your faith with your confession. (Philemon vs.6) And I pray that the fellowship of your faith may become effective through the knowledge of every good thing which is for Christ's sake.

God has begun His work, so from the day of committal, there is no need to ask anymore. Instead, begin to thank Him each day. Repeat each scripture as you apply it to the person for whom you are praying. By doing this, you hold fast to your profession, and believe you have received, even before the evidence appears before you. Do not stop thanking God each day, in each scripture, and you will see the results come forth.

And the door will be opened to you.

Matthew 21:22   And all things you ask in prayer, believing you will receive.

John 14:13   Whatever you ask in My name, that will I do, so that the Father may be glorified in the Son.

Believing vs. Unbelief

Benedictions

	Asking for God's blessing
Numbers 6:24-26	The LORD bless you and keep you! The LORD let his face shine upon you, and be gracious to you! The LORD look upon you kindly and give you peace!
Genesis 31:49	For he said, "May the LORD keep watch between me and thee when we are absent from one another."
Deuteronomy 4:29	Yet there too you shall seek the LORD, your God; and you shall indeed find him when you search after him with your whole heart and your whole soul.
II Corinthians	The grace of the Lord Jesus Christ, and the love of God and the fellowship of the Holy Spirit, be with all of you.
Jude 24-25	Now to Him who is able to keep you from stumbling, and to make you stand in the presence of His glory blameless with great joy, to the only God our Savior through Jesus Christ our Lord, be glory, majesty, dominion and authority, before all time and now and forever. Amen.
I Chronicles 17:27	Now therefore let it please thee to bless the house of they servant, that it may be before thee forever: for thou blessest, O LORD, and it shall be blest forever.

Receive God's Righteousness with the Prayer of Faith

James, the brother of Jesus Christ, tells us in his letter that *the prayer of a righteous man avails much.* James 5:16.

His letter is also very clear that faith; purity of thought, word and deed, lived out in action through our lives reveals that our faith is truly alive in Christ Jesus.

God's idea of righteousness is very different than ours. In Isaiah His word tells us that our self-righteousness is as *filthy rags.*

That is very alarming! James helps clarify that just doing the best we can….is not good enough. In James 2:10 we find that though we were perfect in all but one point of the law, we are as guilty as if we had broken them all.

The good news is that when we have been born-again, we become free from condemnation as a law breaker. Our Father sees the righteousness of His Son, Christ Jesus and applies it to our account. We have an advocate with the Father. If we confess our sins, He is faithful and just to forgive our sins and to declare us ***righteous***. And if we continue to walk in the Light, as He Himself is in the Light, we have fellowship with one another and the blood of Jesus, His Son, cleanses us from all sin. 1John 1:7

Pray a prayer of commitment in faith and trust that God is faithful to His word. He will transform your life from the inside out, as He fashions you as a new creation into the image of His Son. All the old ways will become new, as you walk in His new life that is gifted to you.

Jesus said, "You shall know the truth and the truth shall set you free; and if I make you free, you shall be free indeed." Call on the Lord Jesus Christ in faith. He will never leave you. Tell others to seek Jesus.

Our Unchanging God

Sometimes when bad things happen, as the death of a child, or a bad storm that does great damage, people blame it on God because they can't explain it. They say God is sovereign. Sovereign is a theological word that refers to the unlimited power of God. Yes, God has unlimited power. He can do anything. But He will not do just anything, because God has limited Himself to His own word, the Bible. That makes Him trustworthy!

God is sovereign outside of His Word. God has already said what He will do in many cases. He has already laid out His plan, and it is very clear. God promises in Psalm 89:3-4, not to break or alter His word.

The law and insurance companies, refer to disasters as an act of God. Sometimes religion says that everything good and bad comes from God. It is the Old Testament way of thinking. If that is true, I wonder what Satan is doing. He must not have much to do, if God is sending sickness, killing babies, sending disasters via storms, etc., or withholding healing from believers.

If you believe that God does not always keep his word, then you don't understand the Word of God. But if you believe that God is just, and that He keeps His Word, then sovereignty makes sense. The Bible attests to God's faithfulness to His Word.

Jesus came to call out a people for His own, to tell us the truth about

God and Satan, and to wipe out our sin. He did this to help us see clearly, and to get to know God on a personal level. Jesus redeemed us, and broke the barrier between God and us! Jesus exposed Satan by teaching us that Satan comes to steal, kill, and destroy. Jesus said that He came that we might have life, and have it more abundantly. Jesus is the Good Shepherd. John 10:10-11.

When Jesus started His ministry, He did not waste time exposing the liar. He was not idle while Satan afflicted and tormented people. Jesus had compassion, and he started casting Satan and his demons out. The devil and his demons had been stealing, killing, and destroying since the fall of man. Jesus came to show us how to put a stop to it by rebuking Satan, and casting him out in Jesus' name. Satan cannot read our minds, so we have to cast him out verbally. (Read Luke Chapter 10:1-20)

The Bible states that God's word does not return to God void. But God's word can return to me void if I don't really believe God's word in faith. So there are times when I can stop my own success in receiving from God.

Let's use Mary as an example.

In Luke 1:45 we are told, "Blessed is she who believes that there will be a fulfillment of what has been spoken to her by the Lord." What did Mary believe? She believed the promises the Lord made to her.

But even more, she believed everything that God said about Himself and what He would do. She reasoned that because God had been faithful in the past, He would be faithful in the future. God does not change. He is always faithful. This was the foundation of Mary's life. Above all else, she believed God.

Like Mary, we, too, are called to build our lives on a foundation of God and His promises. Those who trust in God know a joy of heart that confounds the world.

Do you look to God, and take his promises in Scripture as personal promises He is making directly to you? When you meet His conditions, His promises are for your blessing. (See John 15:7)

In prayer, ask God to convince you of His faithfulness. He will give you a peace that passes understanding, and that overcomes worry and temptation.

Our personal experiences do not prove or disprove God's will. There is no question as to whether or not God wants to do something. The question is, "What does God's word say?" God is sovereign outside of His word. His power is unlimited. However, God is true to His word.

Let's take healing, for instance. Healing is a promise in the Bible. When we say, "God is sovereign," as a reason for the person not getting healed, we are actually saying that God broke His word. God will not violate His word. If I lay hands on a sick person, I must have faith in God's promises. The body responds to the mind and the spirit. The body is a vessel for the combination of our spirit and soul.

Love plays a big part in this. In Galatians 5:6, we are told that faith works by love. If we are unforgiving of another person, or sowing seeds of discord, our faith will be stopped from working. Faith is very important in receiving healing power. Love must also be paramount in our lives.

If I don't believe that God heals everyone, then I must not think that He saves everyone who wants salvation. The truth is that salvation is always there, as it is with healing and everything else Jesus died to give us, but it is not always received. Jesus deals with the heart first, and then the body. The heart accepts first, and the body next.

> Whenever something traumatic happens in our lives, our human tendency is to go into a "fight or flight" mode. We think that we have to take some kind of action right away to fix the problem. Sometimes Jesus calls us to be still and we do not recognize the strength there is in waiting on God.
>
> We may be sure that God is true to His word and answers all sincere prayers offered in the name of Jesus Christ. God's answer may be yes, or it may be no, or it may be "wait." If it is no or wait, we cannot say that God has not anwered our prayer. It means that God answered our prayer according to what He knows is best for us, and His answer might be different from what we expected.
>
> We have to remember that God is our loving Father and He does not give His children everything that they ask for. He gives according to His wise and loving will for our lives. But God always answers our prayers.

In Romans 10:9-10, we are assured that God's word is His will!

In Romans 5:9, we are assured that His wrath is not reserved for His own children. We are under His grace because of Jesus' blood. God's wrath is for those who reject Jesus' sacrifice, the ungodly, and the unrighteous. God's wrath comes when the work of sin is finished.

In James 1:15-22, God warns against temptation, and the luring of one's own desire to participate in evil and sin. He tells us not to be deceived, to put away all growth of wickedness, and to "humbly receive the word implanted, which is able to save your souls." He asks us to "prove yourselves doers of the word, and not merely hearers who delude themselves." He speaks of one becoming an "effectual doer" who will be blessed in what they do. Of course, each person has the choice to live different from God's recommendations, and to then suffer the consequences. God allows a person the right to go to hell, if they so choose. God leaves the choice up to each individual. But God prefers us to choose to live the ways He describes. He is that just.

God's love story, the Bible, tells us that our Father God loves us and cares about us. He has gone to great lengths to provide for us. He is our sovereign God, unlimited in His power, and unlimited in His love. See II Peter 3. However, He will not break His word. He promised to keep His promises. That is the kind of God our Father is!! Psalm 89:3-4.

The Bible is truly God's love story. When one reads the Bible, you will know the person of Jesus. John 1:14, states that Jesus is the Word. When a person reads the Bible, they will know the many promises God made to us. When one reads the Bible, they will know their right standing with God! As one reads the Bible, their faith will be growing. Romans 10:17.

Scripture study should be an enjoyment of God, with the knowledge that God wants to share that enjoyment with us. Whenever Scripture is studied, it should build double love, of God, and of neighbor. If it doesn't, we fail to understand what we study.

There are two types of Scripture study – study and sharing. When you do one (study), then you should do the other (share). One reason for sharing with another is that God reveals Himself differently to each person. We will not see the whole picture if we don't share with others.

However, be careful not to share in pride or superiority. Superiority shows up when the sharing or teaching points a finger at someone. At that point, the sharing or teaching becomes negative. Another reason to share is that when I speak to another about what a Scripture means to me, or how I see it being put into operation, the head knowledge I have seems to move 18 inches down to my heart, and it becomes heart knowledge.

Our Story of Praying God's Promises

On November 10, 1998, we took our 17-year-old son, Frank, to the doctor because he was blacking out. The doctor had Frank wear a heart monitor for 24 hours. It was discovered that Frank's heart rate was varying from normal with 39 to 139 beats per minute, and stopping for as much as 3 seconds.

The doctor said Frank would most likely need a pacemaker soon. With that news came the order to meet with a heart specialist at a larger medical clinic in another town nearby. The Holy Spirit was telling us to pray seriously. We had been praying for Frank, and we had placed Frank on the local prayer chain. We also called our friends, Evangelists Ed and Colleen Klein, and they put Frank on their prayer chain.

This time, however, we sat Frank down in a chair to pray with our hands laid on him. We bound Satan in Jesus's name aloud, because Satan cannot read our minds. We forgave all.

This is the prayer we prayed that afternoon:

"Lord God, we come to You this day in the name of Jesus. We praise You, Lord. You are so good, so trustworthy, so perfect. Thank you Father. Thank you Lord Jesus. Thank You Holy Spirit, for our salvation and for all your gifts. We believe, as You say in Mark 11:24, 25, that we will receive all we are asking for. We forgive everyone who has caused us any problems, and we are sorry for causing any problems to anyone else. We are sorry for all our sins, (which we named silently to God.) We thank you, Father God, for forgiving us.

Jesus, you said in Mark 16:18 and James 5:13-15, for Ruth and Joe, who believe in Your Name, to lay hands on our son, Frank, and he will recover. As we lift our son Frank to You, and we lay hands on him, we ask for total restoration of Frank, especially the healing of his heart.

You said in Romans 8:11, "If the Spirit of the one who raised Jesus from the dead dwells in Frank, the one who raised Christ from the dead will give life to Frank's mortal body, also, through His Spirit that dwells in Frank." Jesus we believe you!

Jesus, in Isaiah 53:4, You said, "It was Frank's infirmity that You bore, and Frank's sufferings that You endured." In Isaiah 53:5, You said, "Upon You was the chastisement that makes Frank whole, by your stripes Frank is healed." Lord, we thank you!

Lord Jesus, again in Matthew 8:17, You said, "You took away Frank's infirmities and bore Frank's diseases." Lord Jesus, we thank You for that!

Jesus, You said in I Peter 2: 24, "By your wounds Frank has been healed." And again we thank you!

Jesus, in John 14:12-14 You said, "Truly, truly, I say to you, whoever believes in me, the works that I do, he will do also; and greater works than these he will do, because I am going to the Father. Whatever you ask in my name, I will do, so that the Father may be glorified in the Son. If you ask Me anything in My name, I will do it." Lord Jesus, we thank You!

Psalm 28:6-7. Blessed be the Lord, who has heard the sound of our pleadings. The Lord is Frank's strength and Frank's shield, in which Frank's heart trusts and finds help. So Frank's heart rejoices! With our song we praise our God! Thank you Father for healing Frank. We praise you. We love You. To You be the honor and the glory!

After praying, we drove to the local clinic and picked up a large envelope of x-rays, EKG's and medical records. We proceeded to the large clinic in another town, where we were told that specialists would be waiting for us.

By 4 P.M. we were in the examination room. The cardiologist could not find anything wrong with Frank, so new tests were ordered, and another cardiologist was brought in. Both doctors confirmed that Frank was healthy and normal. We were busy praising God! Frank was busy telling the doctors that God healed him. The doctors also praised God.

An interesting thing happened that morning, we learned later. Two thousand miles away, an old school buddy who had not seen Frank in five years, and who did not know about Frank's health, prayed for God to "walk with Frank" during their family prayer.

God answers prayer!

What About Prayer?

Prayer to me is this—God says it, I hear it, I pray it, and God does it.

Prayer is Jesus Christ praying to the Father through me. He initiates the prayer, I speak it, and the Holy Spirit executes it.

Jesus wants our will to unite with His will. Sometimes we pray for what we have decided we need. We will be happier if we pray for what God knows we need. God governs the whole universe by His Word. God, in His infinite wisdom, is not going to give us anything separate from Jesus Christ. John 1:14, tells us, "And the Word became flesh and made His dwelling among us, and we saw His glory, the glory of the Father's only Son, full of grace and truth."

When we pray for righteousness, He won't give that to us. He gives us Christ, Who is our righteousness. We are co-workers with Christ. God answers prayers based upon the common good. Notice that when you say the Our Father, it is our Father, not my Father. God wants me to think community, so I will know that He won't give me something at someone else's expense.

Prior to prayer, I should forgive all, confess my sins, and thank God for forgiveness. Mark 11:25 says that when I stand to pray, I am to forgive anyone against whom I have a grievance, so that my heavenly Father may, in turn, forgive me my transgressions. I don't dwell on the confession part, because in my humanity, I might bring up old sins that have already been confessed and forgiven, and to confess them again would be unbelief of God's forgiveness. Sometimes Christians try to get back that from which Jesus has set them free.

I like Psalm 50:14,15. It says, "Offer praise as your sacrifice to God; fulfill your vows to the Most High. Then call on me in time of distress; I will rescue you, and you shall honor me." I think how often I forget to offer praise. Sometimes it is easy to take God for granted, and just call on Him when I am in need. Usually what follows in that situation are "give me" prayers. My brother in Christ, Evangelist Ed Klein, reminds me that praise is reminding God who He is, what He has done, and what He is doing. Also, my praise is taking His word back to Him. God doesn't need my praise, but I need to praise Him because:

Praise

Psalms 67:4

Praise Allows God to Guide us
O let the nations be glad and sing for joy;
for thou shall judge the people righteously, and govern the nations upon the earth.

Psalms 22:3-4

Praise Allows God to Rule in and through Us
But thou are Holy, O thou that inhabits the praises of Israel. Our fathers trusted in thee: they trusted, and thou did deliver them.

Psalms 8:2

Praise Stops the Enemy
Out of the mouth of babes and sucklings has thou ordained strength because of thine enemies, that thou might still the enemy and the avenger.

Psalms 8:1	**Praise Establishes God's Power in Us** O LORD our Lord, how excellent is thy name in all the earth! Who hast set thy glory above the heavens.
Psalms 50:23	**Praise Opens a View of God's Salvation for Us** Whoso offers praise glorifies Me: and to him that orders his conversation aright will I show the salvation of God.
Psalms 68:1	**Praise Brings God's Abiding Presence into Focus** Let God arise, let His enemies be scattered; let also them that hate Him flee before Him.
Psalms 149:4	**Praise Brings Pleasure to God from His People** For the LORD takes pleasure in His people: He will beautify the meek with salvation.
Psalms 17:7	**Praise in Oppression Brings God's Victory** Show thy marvelous loving-kindness, O thou that saves by thy right hand them which put their trust in thee from those that rise up against them.

Shouts of Joy Brings Us Out of Bondage

Psalms 105:2	Sing unto Him, sing psalms unto Him: talk ye of all His wondrous works.
Psalms 105:43-44	**Praise Leads Us Into His Providence** And he brought forth His people with joy, and His chosen with gladness; and gave them the lands of the heathen; and they inherited the labor of the people; that they might observe His statutes, and keep His laws. Praise ye the Lord.

Part Two

Faith in Action

Testimonies of God's Love, Faithfulness, and Awesome POWER

"Now to Him that is able to do far more
abundantly beyond all that we ask
or think, according to the
power that works within us,
to Him be the glory in the church
and in Christ Jesus to all
generations forever
and ever.
Amen."
Ephesians 3:20-21

Faith in Action

Healing an Unstable Heart

We had a very special lesson on "Praying God's Promises" with one of our friends in our bible study and prayer group. On one of the nights that we were to meet for study we all began to gather and when it became time to start, we realized that Joe and Rose Rodelo were not with us yet. They were our song leaders and we couldn't start with out praising the Lord in music!

Someone said that they thought that they heard that Joe had a heart attack and was in the hospital. Well….we closed our bibles and put our things away and went over to the local hospital where we found that Joe did indeed have a heart attack and was in the cardiac section. There were about 12 of us that night and we all went into Joe's room. We were really surprised that the head nurse let all of us in. We were told that Joe was getting transferred from that hospital because the doctors could not stabilize his heart.

Our group gathered around Joe and laid hands on him and prayed. We prayed that the Lord would bind Satan in Jesus' Name, and asked God to help us forgive others and confessed our sins to God.

We sang victory songs and prayed God's promises in scripture, especially John chapter 14. We didn't plan any type of prayer service that night, we were just under the direction of the Holy Spirit. The head nurse said we had to leave after we had been there about 45 minutes as the ambulance was there to take Joe to a larger hospital about 50 miles away. All of us went outside in faith and praised God for Joe's healing. Than we all went home.

The next day we went to the hospital where Joe had been moved. We wanted to be with his wife Rose and see how Joe was doing. Well, we were pleasantly surprised how fast God had answered our prayers. The doctors were getting ready to release Joe. They had performed an angiogram and were unable to find anything wrong. Joe's doctor told him he had a very young looking heart!

More than one miracle took place that night at the hospital. It is unheard of that 12 people, all at one time, would be allowed into a cardiac unit room with an unstable heart patient.

During that time that our group was singing songs of praise and worship to the Lord, several other patients and hospital staff members had gathered outside of the room to listen and see what was happening.

As a result of that night, we learned that at least one of the on-lookers soon afterwards had a heart and life changing experience, accepting God's forgiveness for sin, and is now an active follower of Christ Jesus, the Lord.

Our God delights in revealing His love and power to answer His believers' prayers!

Panic, Prayer, and Praise

Praying God's promises became even more real to Joe this past February. We had gone out to the Southwest to vacation for a couple of months in Yuma, Arizona. While we were there, we had traveled to Northern California to visit some friends where we used to live. Also we visited Joe's sister and her family in Sacramento.

After about a week, we headed on our way back to Yuma to spend a little more time in the sun and warm temperatures. On the way back, Joe became very ill.

We had traveled rather late in the evening and had pulled off the highway into a quiet area for the night. In the morning we got up and got ready for the next days' trip. We fully expected to get to Yuma by late afternoon.

Joe got behind the wheel to continue and he had driven about 20 miles or so when be began to get the chills. He said that he was cold, and that he knew that he had a temperature. Soon he was shaking so much that he couldn't drive anymore. So we traded places and I started driving. I asked Joe if he wanted to go to a hospital and he said no at first, and then after a few more miles, Joe said that we should look for one. The next town that we came to, we found a hospital, parked and went in.

Joe was having severe abdominal pains and had already had his appendix removed years earlier. The ER doctor ordered some tests to see what was causing the problem.

I called our daughter back home in Wisconsin to let her know what was happening and asked her to call our two sons and tell them what was going on with their dad. I had called Joe's doctor in Wisconsin too, and he said that he would talk to the doctor that was treating Joe where we were. Our daughter had also called our Pastor and Joe's sisters and some friends and asked for prayer.

Joe had asked the ER doctor if he could go home and was told, "No way! The next place he was going was into surgery!" Joe was told that he had gangrene in his bowel and would need to have surgery to remove it. This diagnosis came after blood work, x-rays and scans had been completed. So Joe went upstairs to wait until the surgeon could make arrangements for the surgery.

The nurse was taking vital signs to admit him to the surgical floor and had a problem getting a reading on Joe's blood pressure. Joe had been hooked up to a monitor and the reading was very low, so the nurse got another monitor to check it and it still was low. She finally went to get a manual blood pressure cuff and the nurse said that Joe's pressure was very low.

The nurse would take his blood pressure every few minutes and it was still low, so Joe was moved back downstairs to the ICCU unit and was hooked up to monitors and IV's. Joe was given medicine to try to lower his temperature from 103.7, and medicine to raise the blood pressure from 67/28. Joe was very sick so the surgeon postponed the surgery until he could get Joe stabilized.

All through the night and into the next day Joe's temperature remained up and his blood pressure was still very low. Joe would have periods where he would lose consciousness. Once when he awoke he said that he could not see, and everything was black. He said that he was aware of a heavy dark presence floating beside him, just off to his right side. I laid my hands on Joe and prayed to the Lord Jesus to kick out Satan and the spirits of darkness. Joe soon rested easier for awhile.

Through out the day Joe had more tests and had more blood work done. The surgeon had called in an internist and they were both talking about doing the surgery but Joe's blood pressure was still too low. In the meantime, I talked to our children and they were making arrangements to come to the hospital.

Saturday night I put a call into our friends, Evangelists Ed and Colleen Klein. Previously, we had helped them for a short time in their ministry. When I told Colleen what was happening she said that she would have Ed call back and talk to Joe. That evening Ed called and while Ed prayed boldly, I laid hands on Joe and prayed in agreement with Ed that Joe would be healed. Ed who is a bold prayer warrior bound the demons in Jesus' name and prayed the promises in scripture for an infilling of health, wholeness, and an immediate total restoration and healing according to the biblical promises.

Joe seemed to rest easier almost immediately and his temperature and blood pressure started to return to normal. By the next morning, Joe felt good again, proclaimed his healing, and said that he was ready to go home!

Joe than underwent more blood work and portable x rays that the doctor ordered. A short while later, the surgeon came in and said, "I don't know what is going on around here, but if you keep acting like this, we will send you home tomorrow." He also told us that surgery was not needed at this time.

Monday morning the doctor scheduled Joe for an MRI and a nuclear scan. Later the doctor came in and told Joe that he was weird, but he did find out two things from the tests. One, Joe did have a brain and two, all he found was a little sinus infection.

Joe was then released from the hospital by a bewildered surgeon, and we proceeded on our way to Yuma. We decided to rest and relax for a few more days before heading back home to Wisconsin.

God Divides the Flames at the Old Gulch Forest Fire

We used to live in California up in the foothills of the Sierra Nevada Mountains. It was beautiful with a view of three different mountains from our place. There were lots of huge old pine trees, manzanita trees, and oak trees all around us. When we bought the property it had two areas where Joe could tell the water was coming down the side of the mountain, so we developed it into a small three acre lake.

He built a small dock and a diving raft for the middle of the lake and leveled off a place a hundred yards long with football goal posts for playing football and throwing around Frisbees. There was a rough path around the lake, but not much else. Joe stocked lots of bluegills and black bass in the lake. Our kids learned to swim and enjoyed fishing there as they were growing up.

Joe's conversion is a whole different story unto itself, for another time. After Joe received forgiveness and salvation in Jesus Christ, we started to get together Friday nights with some of the others from the bible study and prayer group we belonged to. On these Friday nights, some people would bring their instruments to play and we would sing praises and pray. We called it Friday night with Jesus. The get-togethers grew and our house was bulging with a ***faith*** community coming from as far away as Sacramento, about 70 miles away. With the numbers growing we knew we would have to move the meetings outside.

Ephesians 5:19 Sundays sprang up as an outgrowth from our sessions for praise and prayer on Friday nights. Joe decided to work on the area around the lake to develop a suitable site for our outdoors meetings.

He built a pavilion with running water. We had a refrigerator, a small counter area and a couple of cupboards. Joe took the bulldozer and built a nice road around the lake and he made meditation stations where we put small posters up. The posters had a saying or scripture on them with a picture to help start a spiritual reflection. Joe had also made some benches. We put one at each of the stations so that someone could sit and pray or meditate.

We began to meet once a month for a potluck picnic, and we would sing and pray and walk the path around the lake. We called it "Ephesians 5:19 Day".

Ephesians 5:19-20 tells us to address one another in psalms and hymns, and spiritual songs, singing and praying to the Lord in our hearts, giving thanks always, and for everything in the name of our Lord Jesus Christ to God the Father. The day became affectionately known as "3rd Sunday," and was open to everybody.

Our celebrations would start at around noon with prayer, a barbeque, and then we would sing, swim, and play games. There was a lot of sharing and connections made on these days as people walked the meditation trail around the lake and many prayers were said for the needs of those that gathered.

A Christian community was formed and the numbers grew, with the highest attendance at 118. I suppose the average was about 80 people, and for the most part there were seven different denominations participating.

On Sunday, August 16th, 1992, while we were all gathered around and eating we noticed a small plume of smoke rising over one of the hills in back of the lake.

We were talking and saying that we hoped that it wasn't anything serious when we got a phone call from one of our neighbors saying that there was a fire starting and it was going up the hill toward the home of our friends, Robert and Elizabeth Jenkins. Robert and Elizabeth lived high up on a mountain. The view from their place was spectacular! At night you could see all kinds of lights from neighboring towns.

We were all talking about the fire and wondering what we should do when the Holy Spirit did some prompting. Some of us were standing and some were still sitting and all of a sudden Ruth was moved to say, "Children, God calls us to pray in times of trouble." Then we all formed a big circle and joined hands and took turns praying. Ruth prayed for a hedge of protection to be placed around Robert and Elizabeth's house as God's word says in Psalms 32:7. Ruth prayed like this; Lord God, You said in Psalms 32 that you are Robert and Elizabeth's hiding place. You said You will *preserve them from trouble, and You will surround them with a hedge of protection. Then we all prayed with thanksgiving for God's protection.*

Robert and Elizabeth, with great faith and trust in God said that they would stay and finish eating and then go home. In the words of Robert and Elizabeth, a miracle took place that night on the mountain:

"Dear Joe & Ruthie,

It was good to hear from you, and we were blessed to hear you and Ruthie are writing a book about prayer. Your call reminded us how God answers prayers. Getting out the pictures and video of the Old Gulch Fire, reminded us that God heard the prayers of a small group of believers seeking his intervention. God did a miracle that day in Mountain Ranch!

I remember having a good time at the barbeque when we got that call from Suzanne alerting us to the forest fire approaching our home. We prayed, finished lunch and started home.

We were able to get into the area because the fire had just started and the back road was not blocked off yet. We met the CDF Fire Fighters on the road home. They had fled the fire as it began consuming our out buildings. We followed them back up the hill to see what was left.

When we gathered for prayer earlier at Joe and Ruthie's we prayed for safety of the fire fighters and the people in the path of the fire, our home, and most importantly, God's will. We hoped for a miracle but were prepared to accept the worst. No matter what, we believed that God would take care of us.

The fire started down the hill from us and built into a firestorm as it consumed the deep brush and trees moving up the canyon. The CDF Fire Fighters were making a stand on top of the hill at our home when the firestorm crossed the ridge. The inferno was too intense and the fire fighters had to give up on saving our home and flee to safety. Nothing could stand before the raging fire; Nothing human.

As we got nearer, we could see that our out buildings and travel trailer were burnt to the ground and still smoldering. To our amazement our home still stood. The power shed was burnt in spots, our front deck had a 4x4 burned off but our home stood amidst the smoldering ashes. I called for my three young dogs and one by one they appeared through the smoke, unharmed!

God had spared our home and all our animals. The fire fighters declared that the survival of our home was a miracle.

The firestorm turned a huge area behind our home into a safe zone because there was nothing else left to burn. The safe area and the fact that we were already there made it possible to stay.

Over the next 12 hours the fire had changed direction several times, burning a 360 degree path over a half mile in all directions around our home. The pictures show the continued devastation after we got home.

Our home is located in the beautiful remote area surrounded by forest and nature. Before the fire, we used our home for youth and adult retreats and gatherings. After the fire we did re-forestation and over the past 13 years we have seen a young healthy forest grow up from the ashes. We are still able to share our home.

We give Joe and Ruthie permission to use the story, letter, pictures, video, and our names for use in their book on prayer.

God works through His people

The media called this event a phenomenon. We called it a miracle since the fire had come up to the house and parted and went around it on both sides. We have an awesome God.

When you think about it, God's ways are not our ways. Crazy as it seems, why would God want to work His miraculous healing, saving power through or for any of us? Why would He depend on us to preach His Good News? Why would God choose to do His supernatural work for us and through us to bless others?

It seems incredible that God would want to show His power to us and make us His instruments through which His power is manifested to the rest of the world. Our part is to respond with the trust and faith that allows Him to work. Jesus meant it when He said, *"Truly, truly I say unto you, he who believes in Me, the works that I do, he will do also, and greater works than these he will do: because I go to the Father"*. (John 14:12)

What an awesome thought that is! Just as Jesus said to His apostles before He sent them out, trust in God makes this possible. When we look to our heavenly Father, He supplies everything we need.

God has confidence in us because He has provided us with all the grace we need to do His mission. The question is, do we have confidence in God? When someone tells us about an illness, or a situation in their life, pray in faith that they be healed. If you have relationships that are strained, such as in your family, pray and expect miracles in Jesus' name!

God wants His miracles to be a normal part of your life. Have confidence, pray with anticipation and watch as God works in you and through you!

Luke 9:3 says: *And He said unto them,"Take nothing for your journey, neither a staff, or a bag, nor bread, nor money, and even do not have two tunics apiece"*.

Jesus told His disciples not to take anything for their journey, meaning that the disciples could not control the mission Jesus sent them on.

Later on Jesus asked them, *"When I sent you out without a purse, bag, or sandals, did you lack anything"?* They said, *"No, not a thing"*. Luke 22:35

God is the provision for His people

When we only take ***trust*** on life's journey, we not only see God's plan for us, but we also see miracles as we go proclaiming the Good News and curing diseases everywhere. Luke 9:6

Sunday, August 16, 1992
God divides the flames at the Old Gulch Forest Fire – The flames burn around the Jenkins home at Mountain Ranch. Miraculously it was left standing.

He sends us out today to proclaim the kingdom of God, heal the sick, and deal with every situation He leads us into, as He works His good works in and through us. Luke 9:2, and Philippians2:12-13. So **trust** is not just only necessary, it is also the foundation for our mission. If we try to control our lives we will lose them. If we give God control of our lives, we will gain them. Luke 19:24. We must **trust** in God to free us from the compulsion to hold onto the control of our lives. **Trust** allows us to receive God's love, power and provision. *"Trust in Him at all times, O people; pour out your heart before Him; God is a refuge for us"*. Psalms 62:8

(Above thoughts used with permission from: ONE BREAD, ONE BODY - Harvest, August 1 – through September 30th , volume 19, number 5 - Presentation Ministries, Inc., 3230 McHenry, Cincinnati, Ohio 45211)

We find, "One Bread, One Body," to be a valuable source of encouragement for meditation on the sacred Scriptures. For a subscription, they can be reached at: 513-662-5378.

Joseph and Ruth Wesley

Part Three

⤺

Take God at His Word

*"By faith we understand that
the worlds were created by the
Word of God, so that which is seen
was not made out of things
which are visible."*
Hebrews 11:3

*"If you abide in Me, and my words
abide in you, ask whatever you
wish and it will be done
for you."*
John 15:7

God's Promises

God governs His body by His Word (promises) and He calls it a covenant. When I go to God and ask God what I should pray for, God will tell me. I find his promise regarding that, and I pray that promise in Jesus' name. Then the Holy Spirit executes it. The reason I forgive all, and then confess my sins, is that the blood of Jesus cleanses me. Then I can approach the throne room boldly, knowing that I will get what Jesus deserves.

Hebrews 11:6 tells us, "But without faith, it is impossible to please Him." If I am condemning myself, do I have faith before God? Without faith before God, am I pleasing to Him?

I never go to prayer expecting what I deserve. I go to prayer expecting what Jesus deserves, because I go on Jesus' merits, not mine.

Romans 14:22 says, "Keep the faith [that] you have to yourself in the presence of God. Blessed is the one who does not condemn himself for what he approves." When we judge others, we condemn ourselves. Romans 2:1.

When we pray, it's like a court-room scene. (a parable)

We pray to God the Father = Judge

In Jesus' name = Defense Attorney

The Holy Spirit is the doer or enforcer = Bailiff

Satan is the accuser of the brethren = Prosecuting Attorney

Galatians 3:14 God has it rigged. Everything is attained by faith in the promise.
Ephesians 1:3 The relationship part of prayer is to abide in Jesus Christ.
It is the same as putting my trust in Jesus. Then the Holy Spirit empowers me with Reyma (God's Word) and makes it real in my heart. God's Word is spoken in my heart. I am the righteousness of God in Jesus Christ, even though my senses and emotions tell me differently.

If I choose to believe it, Christ will make it real in my heart, and then my emotions will line up with the Word of God.
The Scriptures tell me that everything God has, He put into Christ. He didn't put it anywhere else. So, in whom do I abide? Jesus Christ, as He owns all things. Many Christians are poverty-bound because they don't know what they have in Christ Jesus. They are still praying to receive it. Ephesians 1:18 "May the eyes of your hearts be enlightened, so that you

may know what is the hope of His calling, which are the riches of the glory in His inheritance in the saints and what is the surpassing greatness of His power toward us who believe. Christ Jesus left us a will, and it is called the New Testament.

What good would it be for me to inherit a million dollars, if I never bothered to find out about it? We need to know what our Covenant says, what the Testament says, what we were left in Christ Jesus. Everything was given to Jesus, and we have a right to draw on them. I always have to go to Christ, because Jesus says, "Apart from me, I can do nothing." If I am walking in Christ, if I am walking for the common good, all I have to do is ask for what I need. A very important thing for me to do is to get away from the pride of my intellect, or I will not get very close to God. The intellect is associated with my five senses, and living by senses is not faith. So do not look at the circumstances, look only at what Jesus says in His word. When you go to prayer, and you pray God's promises back to Him, there is a miracle in your mouth!

Some day you will need a miracle from God. They are not only miracles to us. They are God's way of working. It might be for you, or for someone else.

The good news is that you can have that miracle! God is a miracle worker. He recorded many of His miracles in His love story, the Bible. In Malachi 3:6, He said, "Surely I, the Lord, do not change." Then again in Hebrews 13:8, He said, "Jesus Christ is the same yesterday, today, and forever!"

There never has been a day of miracles, but there is a God of Miracles, and He never changes. He is here for us today! How can you receive that miracle? Let's look at the word of God.

In Romans 10:8-10, God says, "The Word is near you, in your mouth and in your heart." (That is the word of faith that we preach.) "For if you confess with your mouth that Jesus is Lord, and believe in your heart that God raised Him from the dead, *you will be saved*. For one believes with the heart, and is so justified; and one confesses with the mouth, and is so saved."

The miracle is in our mouths! The promises of God are good. God says in Isaiah 55:11, "So shall my word be, that (which) goes forth from my mouth. It shall not return to me empty, but it shall accomplish that which I purpose, and prosper in the thing for which I sent it."

God watches over His Word to perform it. God's Word has many promises for us. Say them! Confess them! We all have said many times, I believe God. Yet we must do more than believe in our hearts. Romans 10: 9-10 tells us to confess with our mouths! The promise of God is there. Our God who cannot lie, has given us many promises. Speak those promises out loud. Say them to yourself. Say them to Satan. Say them to the sickness, and to all of your troubles. Confess them in the face of all contrary evidence.

God delights when you put Him in remembrance of His word. God used words to create this world. Words in God's mouth are powerful. His words, confessed by our mouths, are also powerful. When we say, and confess, His word, He brings the miracle to pass! Our miracle is in our mouths. It might not come today, next week, or next month, but it will come.

Now Satan will try to rob us of our miracle. He will try to close our mouths. Satan's first word to us might go like this: "What if it doesn't work?" Satan wants us to doubt. Hebrews 4:16, gives advice. "So let us confidently approach the throne of grace to receive mercy, and to find grace for timely help."

So begin today. Do not doubt. Believe in your heart what God said. Say it out loud constantly, with confidence, and you shall have what you say! Remember, God watches over His work and His Word.

Hindrances blocking Prayer

When you don't feel that you get answers from your prayers, search yourself to see if something is blocking you from receiving what God has promised you.

II Corinthians 13:5 says. Examine yourselves to see whether you are living in faith. Test yourselves. Do you not realize that Jesus Christ is in you?

One of the biggest hindrances to unanswered prayer is:

A. UNFORGIVENESS

I John 1:9	If we confess our sins, He is faithful and righteous to forgive us our sins and cleanse us from all unrighteousness.
Matthew 18:21-22	Then Peter came and said to Him, "Lord, how often shall my brother sin against me, and I forgive him? Up to seven times?" Jesus said to him, "I do not say to you up to seven times, but up to seventy times seven."
Mark 11:25	Whenever you stand praying, forgive if you have anything against anyone, so that your Father who is in heaven will also forgive you your transgressions.
Luke 23:34	Then Jesus said, "Father, forgive them, for they do not know what they are doing."

John 20:23   Whose sins you forgive are forgiven them, and whose sins you retain are retained.

II Corinthians 2:10-11   Whomever you forgive anything, so do I. For indeed what I have forgiven, if I have forgiven anything, has been for you in the presence of Christ, so that we might not be taken advantage of by Satan, for we are not unaware of his purposes.

B. OBEDIENCE

Deuteronomy 5:7   Thou shalt have no other gods before me.

Deuteronomy 5:16   Honour thy father and thy mother, as the LORD thy God hath commanded thee; that thy days may be prolonged, and that it may go well with thee, in the land which the LORD thy God giveth thee.

Deuteronomy 7:26   Neither shalt thou bring an abomination into thine house, lest thou be a cursed thing like it: but thou shalt utterly detest it, and thou shalt utterly abhor it; for it is a cursed thing.

Matthew 22:37-38   He said to him, "You shall love the Lord, your God, with all your heart, with all your soul, and with all your mind. This is the great and foremost commandment. The second is like it. You shall love your neighbor as yourself."

Mark 12:30-31   "You shall love the Lord your God with all your heart, with all your soul, with all your mind, and with all your strength." The second is this: "You shall love your neighbor as yourself. There is no other commandment greater than these."

James 4:17   To one who knows the right thing to do and does not do it, it is a sin.

C. HATE

Proverbs 26:26   Whose hatred is covered by deceit, his wickedness shall be shewed before the whole congregation.

Romans 8:1	There is therefore now no condemnation to them which are in Christ Jesus, who walk not after the flesh but after the Spirit.
I Peter 5:7	Casting all your anxiety on Him, because He cares for you.
I John 2:9-11	The one who says he is in the Light and yet hates his brother is in the darkness until now. The one who loves his brother abides in the Light and there is no cause for stumbling in him. But the one who hates his brother is in the darkness and walks in the darkness, and does not know where he is going because the darkness has blinded his eyes.
I John 3:15	Everyone who hates his brother is a murderer; and you know that no murderer has eternal life abiding in him.

D. DOUBT

Proverbs 3:5-6	Trust in the LORD with all thine heart; and lean not unto thine own understanding. In all thy ways acknowledge him, and he shall direct thy paths.
James 5:15	And the prayer offered in faith will restore the one who is sick, and the Lord will raise him up, and if he has committed sins, they will be forgiven him.
Matthew 8:13	And Jesus said to the centurion, "Go; it shall be done for you as you have believed." And the servant was healed that very moment.
Mark 16:16-18	"He who has believed and has been baptized shall be saved; but he who has disbelieved shall be condemned. "These signs will accompany those who have believed: in My name they will cast out demons, they will speak with new tongues; they will pick up serpents, and if they drink any deadly poison, it will not hurt them; they will lay hands on the sick, and they will recover."

John 7:38	"He who believes in me, as the scripture said, From his innermost being will flow rivers of living water."
Romans 4: 20-21	Yet, with respect to the promise of God, he did not waiver in unbelief but grew strong in faith, giving glory to God, and being fully assured that what God had promised, He was able also to perform.
Hebrews 3:12	Take care, brethren, that there not be in any one of you an evil, unbelieving heart that falls away from the living God.
Hebrews 11:1	Now faith is the assurance of things hoped for.

E. UNREPENTED SIN

Genesis 3:3	But of the fruit of the tree which is in the midst of the garden, God hath said, Ye shall not eat of it, neither shall ye touch it, lest ye die.
Psalms 19:12-14	Who can understand his errors? Cleanse thou me from secret faults. Keep back thy servant also from presumptuous sins; let them not have dominion over me: then shall I be upright, and I shall be innocent from the great transgression. Let the words of my mouth, and the meditation of my heart, be acceptable in thy sight, O LORD, my strength, and my redeemer.
Psalms 66:18	If I regard iniquity in my heart, the Lord will not hear me.
Isaiah 59:1-2	Behold, the LORD's hand is not shortened, that it cannot save; neither his ear heavy, that it cannot hear: But your iniquities have separated between you and your God, and your sins have hid his face from you, that he will not hear.
Hebrews 10:26-27	For if we go on sinning willfully after receiving the knowledge of the truth, there no longer remains a sacrifice for sins, but a terrifying expectation of

	judgment and THE FURY OF A FIRE WHICH WILL CONSUME THE ADVERSARIES.
Revelation 2:17	'He who has an ear, let him hear what the Spirit says to the churches. To him that overcomes, to him will I give some of the hidden manna, and I will give him a white stone and a new name written on the stone which no one knows but he who receives it.'
Revelation 3:20	'Behold, I stand at the door and knock; if anyone hears My voice and opens the door, I will come in to him and will dine with him and he with Me.'

F. PRAYING CORRECTLY

Isaiah 55:11	So shall my word be that goeth forth out of my mouth: it shall not return unto me void, but it shall accomplish that which I please, and it shall prosper in the thing whereto I sent it.
Psalms 100:4	Enter into his gates with thanksgiving, and into his courts with praise: be thankful unto him, and bless his name.
John 15:7	"If you abide in Me, and My words abide in you, ask whatever you wish, and it will be done for you."
Ephesians 5:20-21	Always giving thanks for all things in the name of our Lord Jesus Christ to God, even the Father; and be subject to one another in the fear of Christ.
Philippians 4:6	Be anxious for nothing, but in everything by prayer and supplication with thanksgiving let your requests be known to God.
I Thessalonians 5:17-18	Pray without ceasing; in everything give thanks; for this is God's will for you in Christ Jesus.

G. TEMPLE OF GOD

I Corinthians 3:16	Do you not know that you are a temple of God and that the Spirit of God dwells in you?

I Corinthians 6:19	Or do you not know that your body is the temple of the Holy Spirit who is in you, whom you have from God, and that you are not your own?
Luke 21:34	"Be on guard, so that your hearts will not be weighted down with dissipation and drunkenness and the worries of life, and that day will not come on you suddenly like a trap."
Romans 12:1-2	Therefore I urge you, brethren, by the mercies of God, to present your bodies a living and holy sacrifice, acceptable to God, which is your spiritual service of worship. And do not be conformed to this world, but be transformed by the renewing of your mind, so that you may prove what the will of God is, that which is good and acceptable and perfect.

H. TOUCHING GOD'S ANOINTED

Psalms 105:14-15	He suffered no man to do them wrong: yea, he reproved kings for their sakes saying, Touch not mine anointed, and do my prophets no harm.
I Samuel 26:9	And David said to Abishai, Destroy him not: for who can stretch forth his hand against the LORD'S anointed, and be guiltless?
I Corinthians 12:28	And God has appointed in the church, first apostles, second prophets, third teachers, then miracles, then gifts of healings, helps, administrations, various kinds of tongues.
Ephesians 4:11	And He gave some as apostles, and some as prophets, and some as evangelists, and some as pastors and teachers.
I Thessalonians 5:12	But we request of you, brethren, that you appreciate those who diligently labor among you, and have charge over you in the Lord and give you instruction.

Hebrews 6:10	For God is not unjust so as to forget your work and the love you have shown toward His name, in having ministered and in still ministering to the saints.

I. FEAR

Isaiah 51:7	Hearken unto me, ye that know righteousness, the people in whose heart is my law; fear ye not the reproach of men, neither be ye afraid of their revilings.
Psalms 111:10	The fear of the LORD is the beginning of wisdom: a good understanding have all they that do his commandments: his praise endureth for ever.
Proverbs 2:5	Then shalt thou understand the fear of the LORD, and find the knowledge of God.
Proverbs 29:25	The fear of man bringeth a snare: but who so putteth his trust in the LORD shall be safe.
Malachi 3:16	Then they that feared the LORD spake often one to another; and the LORD hearkened, and heard it, and a book of remembrance was written before him for them that feared the LORD, and that thought upon his name.
II Timothy 1:7	For God has not given us a spirit of timidity, but of power and love and discipline.
I John 4:18	There is no fear in love; but perfect love casts out fear, because fear involves punishment, and the one who fears is not perfected in love.

J. ROBBING GOD OF HIS TITHES

Malachi 3: 8	Will a man rob God? Yet ye have robbed me. But ye say, Wherein have we robbed thee? In tithes and offerings.
Leviticus 27:30-31	And all the tithe of the land, whether of the seed of the land, or of the fruit of the tree, is the LORD'S: it is holy unto the LORD. And if a man will at all redeem ought of his tithes, he shall add thereto the fifth part thereof.

Joshua 6:19	But all the silver, and gold, and vessels of brass and iron, are consecrated unto the LORD: they shall come into the treasury of the LORD.
Proverbs 3:9	Honour the LORD with thy substance, and with the firstfruits of all thine increase:
Luke 6:38	"Give and it will be given to you. They will pour into your lap a good measure-pressed down, shaken together, and running over. For by your standard of measure it will be measured to you in return."
Romans 12:13	Contributing to the needs of the saints, practicing hospitality.
I Corinthians 9:13	Do you not know that those who perform sacred services eat the food of the temple, and those who attend regularly to the altar have their share from the altar?
II Corinthians 9:6-10	Now this I say, he who sows sparingly will also reap sparingly, and he who sows bountifully will also reap bountifully. Each one must do as he has purposed in his heart, not grudgingly or of compulsion, for God loves a cheerful giver. And God is able to make all grace abound to you, so that always having all sufficiency in everything, you may have an abundance for every good deed; as it is written, "HE SCATTERED ABROAD, HE GAVE TO THE POOR, HIS RIGHTEOUSNESS ENDURES FOREVER."

K. EXAMINATION BEFORE RECEIVING COMMUNION

I Corinthians 11:27-31	Therefore whoever eats the bread or drinks the cup of the Lord in an unworthy manner, shall be guilty of the body and the blood of the Lord. But a man must examine himself, and in so doing he is to eat of the bread and drink of the cup. For he who eats and drinks, eats and drinks judgment to himself if he does not judge the body

rightly. For this reason many among you are weak and sick, and a number sleep. But if we would judge ourselves rightly, we would not be judged.

Ephesians 4:29-32   Let no unwholesome word proceed from your mouth, but only such a word as is good for edification according to the need of the moment, so that it will give grace to those who hear. Do not grieve the Holy Spirit of God by whom you were sealed for the day of redemption. Let all bitterness and wrath and anger and clamor and slander be put away from you, along with all malice. Be kind one to another, tender- hearted, forgiving each other, just as God in Christ also has forgiven you.

Galatians 5:26   Let us not become boastful, challenging one another, envying one another.

Romans 15:5-6   Now may the God who gives perseverance and encouragement grant you to be of the same mind with one another according to Christ Jesus so that with one accord you may with one voice glory the God and Father of our Lord Jesus Christ.

Hebrews 10:23-24   Let us hold fast the confession of our hope without wavering, for He who promised is faithful; and let us consider how to stimulate one another to love and good deeds.

James 4:11   Do not speak against one another, brethren. He who speaks against a brother or judges his brother, speaks against the law and judges the law; but if you judge the law, you are not a doer of the law but a judge of it.

L. FAITH

Romans 10:17   So faith comes from hearing, and hearing by the word of Christ.

Matthew 9:29   Then He touched their eyes, saying, "It shall be done to you according to your faith."

Mark 5:34	And He said to her, "Daughter, your faith has made you well; go in peace and be healed of your affliction."
Luke 1:45	"And blessed is she who believed that there would be a fulfillment of what had been spoken to her by the Lord."
Romans 4:20	Yet, with respect to the promise of God, he did not waiver in unbelief but grew strong in faith, giving glory to God.
Hebrews 10:23	Let us hold fast the confession of our hope without wavering, for He who promised is faithful.
Luke 22:41-42	And He withdrew from them about a stone's throw, and He knelt down and began to pray, saying, "Father if you are willing, remove this cup from Me; yet not my will, but yours be done."
Mark 14:36	And He was saying, "Father; if you are willing, remove this cup from Me; yet not My will, but Yours be done."

M. TIME TO DIE

Isaiah 55:6	Seek ye the LORD while he may be found, call ye upon him while he is near:
Hebrews 9:27	And inasmuch as it is appointed for men to die once and after this comes judgment.

N. CONDITIONS

Job 3:25	For the thing which I greatly feared is come upon me, and that which I was afraid of is come unto me.
Job 22:28	Thou shalt also decree a thing, and it shall be established unto thee: and the light shall shine upon thy ways.

ABSENTMINDEDNESS

Proverbs 16:3	Commit thy works unto the LORD, and thy thoughts shall be established.
Isaiah 50:7	For the LORD GOD will help me; therefore shall I not be confounded: therefore have I set my face like a flint, and I know that I shall not be ashamed.
John 14:26	"But the Helper, the Holy Spirit, whom the Father will send in My name, He will teach you all things, and bring to your remembrance all that I said to you.
I Corinthians 2:16	For who has known the mind of the Lord, that He will instruct Him? But we have the mind of Christ.
II Timothy 1:5-7	For I am mindful of the sincere faith within you, which first dwelt in your grandmother Lois and your mother Eunice, and I am sure that it is in you as well. For this reason I remind you to kindle afresh the gift of God which is in you through the laying on of my hands. For God has not given us a spirit of timidity, but of power and love and discipline.

AFFLICTIONS

Job 23:10	But He knows the way I take; when He has tried me I shall come forth as gold.
Job 36:15	He delivereth the poor in His affliction, and opened their ears in oppression.
Psalm 25:18	Look upon mine affliction and my pain; and forgive all my sins.
Psalm 28:7	The LORD is my strength and my shield; my heart trusted in Him, and I am helped; therefore my heart greatly rejoiceth; and with my song will I praise Him.

Psalms 31:16	Make Thy face to shine upon Thy servant: save me for thy mercies sake.
Psalms 34:18	Behold, the eye of the LORD is upon them that fear Him, upon them that hope in His mercy.
Psalms 56:11	In GOD have I put my trust: I will not be afraid what man can do unto me.
Psalms 119:50	This is my comfort in my affliction: for Thy word hath quickened me.
Psalms 119:71	It is good for me that I have been afflicted; that I may learn Thy statutes.
Psalms 119:107	I am afflicted very much: quicken me, O LORD, according unto thy word.
Psalms 119:153	Consider mine affliction, and deliver me: for I do not forget thy law.
Isaiah 49:13	Sing, O heavens; and be joyful, O earth; and break forth into singing, O mountains; for the LORD hath comforted His people, and will have mercy upon His afflicted.

ANGER

Job 5:2	For wrath killeth the foolish man, and envy slayeth the silly man.
Psalms 18:48-49	He delivereth me from my enemies: yea, thou liftest me up above those that rise up against me: thou hast delivered me from the violent man. Therefore will I give thanks unto thee, O LORD, among the heathen and sing praises unto thy name.

ANXIETY

Psalms 107:19	Then they cry unto the LORD in their trouble, and He saveth them out of their distresses.

Proverbs 12:25	Heaviness in the heart of man maketh it to stoop: but a good word maketh it glad.
Matthew 28:19-20	"Go therefore and make disciples of all the nations, baptizing them in the name of the Father and the Son and the Holy Spirit, teaching them to observe all that I command you; and lo, I am with you always even unto the end of the age."
Luke 12:11-12	When they bring you before the synagogues and the rulers and the authorities, do not worry about what or how you are to speak in your defense, or what you are to say; for the Holy Spirit will teach you in that very hour what you ought to say."
Philippians 4:6-7	Be anxious for nothing, but in everything by prayer and supplication with thanksgiving let your requests be made known to God. And the peace of God, which surpasses all comprehension, will guard your hearts and minds in Christ Jesus.
I Peter 5:7	Casting all your care on Him, because He cares for you.

ASKING GOD

Psalms 2:8	Ask of me and I shall give thee the heathen for thine inheritance, and the uttermost parts of the earth for thy possession.
Psalms 4:4	I cried unto the LORD with my voice, and he heard me out of His holy hill.
Psalms 20:1	The LORD hear thee in the day of trouble; the name of the God of Jacob defend thee;
Psalms 20:5	We will rejoice in thy salvation, and in the name of our God we will set up our banners: the LORD fulfill all thy petitions.

Matthew 6:33 "But seek first His kingdom and His righteousness, and all these things will be added to you."

Matthew 7:8 "Ask and it will be given to you; seek, and you will find; knock and it will be opened to you. For everyone who asks receives, and he who seeks finds, and to him who knocks it will be opened."

BINDING AND LOOSENING

Satan can be bound in the name of Jesus. Spiritual warfare is hard to understand in the natural, because we cannot see whom we are fighting. We must remember that we are fighting against powers and principalities. Since Satan can't read our minds, we must bind him in the name of Jesus audibly.

Binding and loosening is a command. It is building the Church away from the power of Satan into the power of Jesus. Whenever you bind Satan and his spirits of darkness and evil, you must name the unclean spirit by name: sickness, doubt, envy, pain, and suffering, etc. Now you must loose the power of heaven in Jesus' name and ask for an infilling of the Holy Spirit i.e.; health, healing, confidence, wholeness, restoration, love, joy, peace, etc., so there is no room for unclean spirits to return, because Luke 11:24-26 tells us, "When an unclean spirit goes out of someone, it roams through arid regions searching for rest, but finding none, it says 'I shall return to my home from which I came.' But upon returning it finds it swept clean and put in order. Then it goes and brings back seven other spirits more wicked than itself who move in and dwell there, and the last condition of that person is worse than the first."

Be sure to give glory and praise to God for the ability you have to be able to bind up all the powers of darkness. (Read Luke, chapter 10) Whatever the unclean spirit is, ask God to show you, so that you can recognize it and name it. He will help you to discern what it is that is attacking you, and He will help you bind it. Just be sure to say it out loud in Jesus' name.

Ephesians 1:19-23 And what is the surpassing greatness of His power toward us who believe. These are in accordance with the working of the strength of His might which He brought about in Christ Jesus, when He raised Him from the dead and seated Him at His right hand in the heavenly places, far above all rule and authority and power and dominion, and every name that is named, not only in this age but also in the one to come. And

	He put all things in subjection under His feet, and gave Him as head over all things to the church, which is His body, the fullness of Him who fills all in all.
Ephesians 2:4-10	But God, being rich in mercy, because of His great love with which He loved us, even when we were dead in our transgressions, made us alive together with Christ (by grace you have been saved), and raised us up with Him, and seated us with Him in heavenly places in Christ Jesus, so that in the ages to come He might show the surpassing riches of His grace in kindness toward us in Christ Jesus. For by grace you have been saved through faith; and that not of yourselves, it is the gift of God; not as a result of works, so that no one may boast. For we are His workmanship, created in Christ Jesus for good works, which God prepared beforehand so that we would walk in them.
Luke 10:19	"Behold, I have given you authority to tread on serpents and scorpions, and over all the power of the enemy, and nothing will injure you."
Mark 3:26-27	If Satan has risen up against himself and is divided, he cannot stand; but he is finished! But no one can enter the strong man's house and plunder his property unless he first binds the strong man, and then he can plunder his house.
John 14:13-14	Whatever you ask in My name, that will I do, so that the Father may be glorified in the Son. If you ask Me anything in My name, I will do it.
Matthew 18:18-20	"Truly I say unto you, whatever you bind on earth shall be bound in heaven; and whatever you loose on earth shall be loosed in heaven. Again, I say to you, that if two of you on earth agree upon anything that they may ask, it shall be done for them by My Father who is in heaven. For where two or three are gathered in My name, I am there in their midst."

Before praying a binding and loosening prayer for someone, be sure to ask for their permission first. Be careful not to place your judgement on anyone. Trust God and His word, His promises are sure.

By your example of words and actions tell the people about God's grace, mercy and forgiveness through experiences in your life. Your belief and trust in God's Word will draw them more quickly into acceptance of God's will.

Be always ready to use binding and loosening in your own lives.

Child Training

Proverbs 3:11-12	My son, despise not the chastening of the LORD; neither be weary of his correction: For whom the LORD loveth he correcteth; even as a father the son in whom he delighteth.
Proverbs 22:6	Train up a child in the way he should go: and when he is old, he will not depart from it.
Proverbs 29:15	The rod and reproof give wisdom: for the child left to himself bringeth his mother to shame.
Proverbs 29:17	Correct thy son, and he shall give thee rest; he shall give delight unto thy soul.
Colossians 3:21	Fathers, do not exasperate your children, so that they will not loose heart.
Deuteronomy 6:6-7	And these words, which I command thee this day, shall be in thine heart: And thou shalt teach them diligently unto thy children, and shalt talk of them when thou sittest in thine house, and when thou walkest by the way, and when thou liest down, and when thou risest up.
Isaiah 54:13	And all thy children shall be taught of the LORD, and great shall be the peace of thy children.

Comfort in Disappointments

Psalms 34:17-18 — The righteous cry, and the LORD heareth, and delivereth them out of all their troubles. The LORD is nigh unto them that are of a broken heart; and saveth such as be of a contrite spirit.

Psalms 55:22 — Cast thy burden upon the LORD, and he shall sustain thee: He shall never suffer the righteous to be moved.

Psalms 94:19 — In the multitude of my thoughts within me thy comforts delight my soul.

Ecclesiastes 9:11 — I return and saw under the sun, that the race is not to the swift, nor the battle to the strong, neither yet bread to the wise, nor riches to men of understanding, nor yet favor to men of skill; but time and chance happeneth to them all.

Isaiah 57:18 — I have seen his ways, and will heal him: I will lead him also, and restore comforts unto him and to mourners.

Isaiah 66:13 — As one whom his mother comforteth, so will I comfort you; and ye shall be comforted in Jerusalem.

Jeremiah 31:13 — Then shall the virgin rejoice in the dance, both young men and old together: for I will turn their mourning into joy, and will comfort them, and make them rejoice from their sorrow.

II Corinthians 1:4-5 — Who comforts us in all our affliction so that we will be able to comfort those who are in any affliction with the comfort with which we ourselves are comforted by God.

II Thessalonians 3:16 — Now may the Lord of peace Himself continually grant you peace in every circumstance. The Lord be with you all!

Comfort for Mourners

Psalms 34:18	The LORD is nigh unto them that are of a broken heart; and saveth such as be of a contrite spirit.
Psalms 147:3	He healeth the broken in heart, and bindeth up their wounds.
Isaiah 53:4	Surely he hath born our grief and carried our sorrows: yet we did esteem him stricken, smitten of God, and afflicted.
Isaiah 57:15	For thus saith the high and lofty One that inhabits eternity, whose name is Holy; I dwell in the high and holy place, with him also that is of a contrite and humble spirit, to revive the spirit of the humble, and to revive the heart of the contrite ones.
Isaiah 61:3	To appoint unto them that mourn in Zion, to give unto them beauty for ashes, the oil of joy for mourning, the garment of praise for the spirit of heaviness; that they might be called trees of righteousness, the planting of the LORD, that he might be glorified.
I Thessalonians 4:13-14	But we do not want you to be uninformed, brethren, about those who are asleep, so that you will not grieve as do the rest who have no hope. For if we believe that Jesus died and rose again, even so God will bring with Him those who have fallen asleep in Jesus.

Condemnation

Revelation 12:10	Then I heard a loud voice in heaven, saying, "Now the salvation and the power, and the kingdom of our God and the authority of His Christ have come, for the accuser of our brethren has been thrown down, he who accuses them before our God day and night.

Romans 5:16	The gift is not like that which came through the one who sinned; for on the one hand the judgment arose from one transgression resulting in condemnation, but on the other hand the free gift arose from many transgressions resulting in justification.
Romans 8:1-2	Therefore there is no condemnation for those who are in Christ Jesus. For the law of the Spirit of life in Christ Jesus has set you free from the law of sin and death.
Romans 14:22	The faith which you have, have as your own conviction before God. Happy is he who does not condemn himself in what he approves.
John 3:17	For God did not send the Son into the world to judge the world, but that the world might be saved through Him.
I John 3:19-21	We will know by this that we are of the truth, and will assure our heart before Him in whatever our heart condemns us; for God is greater than our heart and knows all things. Beloved, if our heart does not condemn us, we have confidence before God.

Confession/Reconciliation

Psalms 32:5	I acknowledged my sin unto thee, and mine iniquity have I not hid. I said, I will confess my transgressions unto the LORD; and thou forgave the iniquity of my sin.
Psalms 51:1-19	Have mercy upon me, O God, according to thy loving kindness; according unto the multitude of thy tender mercies blot out my transgressions. Wash me thoroughly from mine iniquity, and cleanse me from my sin. For I acknowledge my transgressions: and my sin is ever before me. Against thee, thee only, have I sinned, and done this evil in thy sight so that thou might be justified when thou speakest, and be clear when thou judgest. Behold, I was shapen in iniquity; and in sin did my mother con-

ceive me. Behold, thou desirest truth in the inward parts: and in the hidden part thou shalt make me to know wisdom. Purge me with hyssop, and I shall be clean: wash me, and I shall be whiter than snow. Make me to hear joy and gladness; that the bones which thou hast broken may rejoice. Hide thy face from my sins, and blot out all mine iniquities. Create in me a clean heart, O God; and renew a right spirit in me. Cast me not away from thy presence; and take not thy Holy Spirit from me. Restore unto me the joy of thy salvation: and uphold me with thy free spirit. Then will I teach transgressors thy ways; and sinners shall be converted unto thee. Deliver me from bloodguiltiness, O God, thou God of my salvation: and my tongue shall sing aloud of thy righteousness. O Lord, open thou my lips, and my mouth shall shew forth thy praise. For thou desirest not sacrifice; else would I give it: thou delightest not in burnt offering. The sacrifices of God are a broken spirit: a broken and contrite heart, O God, thou wilt not despise. Do good in thy good pleasure unto Zion: build thou the walls of Jerusalem. Then shalt thou be pleased with the sacrifices of righteousness, with burnt offering and whole burnt offering: then shall they offer bullocks upon thine altar.

Psalms 139:23-24	Search me, O God, and know my heart: try me, and know my thoughts and see if there be any wicked way in me, and lead me in the way everlasting.
Proverbs 28:13	He that covers his sins shall not prosper: but whoso confesseth and forsaketh them shall have mercy.
Isaiah 55:6-7	Seek ye the Lord while he may be found, call ye upon him while he is near: let the wicked forsake his way, and the unrighteous man his thoughts: and let him return unto the Lord, and He will have mercy upon him; and to our God, for He will abundantly pardon.

Romans 14:11-12	For it is written, "AS I LIVE, SAYS THE LORD, EVERY KNEE SHALL BOW TO ME, AND EVERY TONGUE SHALL GIVE PRAISE TO GOD." So then each one of us will give an account of himself to God.
James 5:16	Therefore, confess your sins to one another, and pray for one another so that you may be healed. The effective prayer of a righteous man can accomplish much.
I John 1:9	If we confess our sins, He is faithful and righteous to forgive us our sins and to cleanse us from all unrighteousness.

Confidence

Exodus 23:25	And ye shall serve the LORD your God, and he shall bless thy bread, and thy water; and I will take sickness away from the midst of thee.
Psalms 37:3-4	Trust in the LORD, and do good; so shalt thou dwell in the land, and verily thou shalt be fed. Delight thyself in the LORD; and he shall give thee the desires of thine heart.
Psalms 46:2	Therefore will not we fear though the earth be removed, and though the mountains be carried into the midst of the sea.
Psalms 119:89	Forever, O LORD, thy word is settled in heaven.
Isaiah 30:15	For thus saith the LORD GOD, the Holy One of Israel; In returning and rest shall ye be saved; quietness and in confidence shall be your strength: and ye would not.
Isaiah 58:8	Then shall thy light break forth as the morning, and thine health shalt spring forth speedily: and thy righteousness shall go before thee; the glory of the LORD shall be thy rereward.(rear guard)

Proverbs 3:5-6	Trust in the LORD with all thine heart; and lean not unto thine own understanding. In all thy ways acknowledge him, and he shall direct thy paths.
Proverbs 3:26	For the LORD shall be thy confidence, and shall keep thy foot from being taken.
Proverbs 14:26	In the fear of the LORD is strong confidence; and his children shall have a place of refuge.
Proverbs 19:23	The fear of the LORD tendeth to life: and he that hath it shall abide satisfied; he shall not be visited with evil.
John 14:26	"But the Helper, the Holy Spirit, whom the Father will send in My name, He will teach you all things and bring to your remembrance all that I said to you."
John 16:13	"But when He, the Spirit of truth, comes, He will guide you into all the truth; for He will not speak on His own initiative, but whatever He hears, will speak; and He will disclose to you what is to come.
Romans 8:11	But if the Spirit of Him who raised Jesus from the dead dwells in you, He who raised Christ Jesus from the dead will also give life to your mortal bodies through His Spirit who dwells in you.
Philippians 1:6	For I am confident of this very thing, that He who began good work in you will perfect it until the day of Christ Jesus.
Hebrews 10:35	Therefore, do not throw away your confidence, which has a great reward.
I Peter 5:7	Cast all your anxiety on Him, because He cares for you.
I John 5:14-15	This is the confidence which we have before Him, that, if we ask anything according to His will, He hears us. And if we know that He hears us in what-

	ever we ask, we know that we have the requests which we have asked from Him.
II Peter 1:3	Seeing that His divine power has granted to us everything pertaining to life and godliness, through the true knowledge of Him who called us by His own glory and excellence.

Confusion

Psalms 20:1-2	The LORD hear thee in the day of trouble; the name of the God of Jacob defend thee; send thee help from the sanctuary, and strengthen thee out of Zion.
Psalms 22: 5-6	They cried unto thee, and were delivered: they trusted in thee, and were not confounded. But I am a worm and no man; a reproach of men, and despised of the people.
Psalms 71:1-3	In thee, O LORD, do I put my trust: Let me never be put to confusion. Deliver me in thy righteousness, and cause me to escape: incline thine ear unto me, and save me. Be though my strong habitation whereunto I may continually resort: thou has given commandment to save me, for thou art my rock and my fortress.
Isaiah 50:7	For the Lord God will help me; therefore shall I not be confounded: therefore have I set my face like a flint, and I know that I shall not be ashamed.
James 5:8	You too be patient; strengthen your hearts, for the coming of the Lord is near.

Counseling

Humanistic counsel cannot produce spiritual results.

Psalms 1:1	BLESSED is the man that walketh not in the counsel of the ungodly, nor standeth in the way of sinners, nor sitteth in the seat of the scornful.

Proverbs 12:5	The thoughts of the righteous are right: but the counsels of the wicked are deceit.
Proverbs 21:30	There is no wisdom nor understanding nor counsel against the LORD.
Proverbs 28:5	Evil men understand not judgment: but they that seek the LORD understand all things.

Death

Psalms 23:4	Yea, though I walk through the valley of the shadow of death, I will fear no evil: for thou art with me; thy rod and thy staff they comfort me.
Psalms 116:15	Precious in the sight of the LORD is the death of his saints.
John 5:21	"For just as the Father raises the dead and gives them life, even so the Son also gives life to whom He wishes."
John 5:24-25	"Truly, truly, I say to you, he who hears My word, and believes Him who sent Me, has eternal life, and does not come into judgment, but has passed out of death into life. "Truly, truly, I say to you, an hour is coming and now is, when the dead will hear the voice of the Son of God, and those who hear will live.
John 5;28	Do not marvel at this, for an hour is coming, in which all who are in the tombs will hear His voice.
John 11:25-6	Jesus said to her, "I am the resurrection and the life; he who believes in Me even if he dies, will live, and everyone who lives and believes in Me will never die. Do you believe this?"
I Corinthians 15:53-54	For this corruptible must put on incorruption, and

this mortal must put on immortality. So when this shall have put on incorruption, and this shall have put on immortality, then shall be brought to pass the saying that is written, "Death is swallowed up in victory."

I Corinthians 15:56-57
The sting of death is sin, and the power of sin is the law; but thanks be to God, who gives us the victory through our Lord Jesus Christ.

II Corinthians 5:8
We are of good courage, I say, and prefer rather to be absent from the body and to be at home with the Lord.

Philippians 1:21
For to me, to live is Christ, and to die is gain.

Hebrews 9:27-28
And inasmuch as it is appointed for human beings to die once, and after this comes judgment, so Christ, also having been offered once to bear the sins of many, will appear a second time for salvation, without reference to sin, to those who eagerly await Him.

Hebrews 2:14-15
Therefore, since the children share in flesh and blood, He Himself likewise also partook of the same, that through death He might render powerless him who had the power of death, that is, the devil, and might free those who, through fear of death, were subject to slavery all their lives.

Deliverance from Addictions

Job 36:15
He delivereth the poor in his affliction, and openeth their ears in oppression.

Psalms 5:2
Hearken unto the voice of my cry, my King and my God: For unto thee will I pray.

Psalms 31:2-5
Bow down thy ear to me; deliver me speedily: be thou my strong rock, for an house of defense to save me. For thou art my rock and my fortress; therefore for thy name's sake lead me, and guide me. Pull me out

	of the net that they have laid privily for me: for thou art my strength. Into thine hand I commit my spirit: thou hast redeemed me, O LORD GOD of truth.
Psalms 34:18	The Lord is nigh unto them that are of a broken heart; and saveth such as be of a contrite spirit.
Psalms 46:1	God is our refuge and strength, a very present help in trouble.
Psalms 55:15-18	Let death seize upon them, and let them go down quick into hell: for wickedness is in their dwellings, and among them. As for me, I will call upon God; and the LORD shall save me. Evening, and morning, and at noon, will I pray, and cry aloud: and He shall hear my voice. He hath delivered my soul in peace from the battle that was against me: for there were many with me.
Psalms 91:3	Surely He shall deliver thee from the snare of the fowler, and from the noisome pestilence.
Psalms 107:6	Then they cried unto the LORD in their trouble, and He delivered them out of their distresses.
Psalms 143:11	Quicken me, O LORD, for thy name's sake: for thy righteousness' sake bring my soul out of trouble.
Psalms 144:7	Send thy hand from above; rid me, and deliver me out of great waters, from the hand of strange children.
Proverbs 11:8	The righteous is delivered out of trouble, and the wicked cometh in his stead.
Isaiah 33:2	O LORD, be gracious with us; we have waited for thee: be thou their arm every morning, our salvation also in the time of trouble.

Jeremiah 15:21	And I will deliver thee out of the hand of the wicked, and I will redeem thee out of the hand of the terrible.
Joel 2:32	And it shall come to pass, that whosoever shall call on the name of the LORD shall be delivered: for in mount Zion and in Jerusalem shall be deliverance, as the LORD hath said, and in the remnant whom the LORD shall call.
Matthew 12:28	"But if I cast out demons by the Spirit of God, then the kingdom of God has come upon you."
Matthew 8:16	When evening came, they brought to Him many who were demon possessed; and He cast out the spirits with a word, and healed all who were ill.
Matthew 18:18	"Truly I say to you, whatever you bind on earth shall have been bound in heaven; and whatever you loose on earth shall be loosed in heaven.
Mark 11:23	"Truly I say to you, whoever says to this mountain, 'Be taken up and cast into the sea,' and does not doubt in his heart, but believes what he says is going to happen, it will be granted him."
Luke 9:1-2	And He called the twelve together, and gave them power and authority over all the demons and to heal diseases. And He sent them out to proclaim the kingdom of God and to perform healing.
Luke 10:19	"Behold, I have given you authority to tread on serpents and scorpions, and over all the power of the enemy, and nothing will injure you."
Acts 10:38	You know of Jesus of Nazareth, how God anointed Him with the Holy Spirit and with power, and how He went about doing good and healing all who were oppressed by the devil, for God was with Him.

Romans 10:10	For with the heart a person believes, resulting in righteousness, and with the mouth he confesses, resulting in salvation.
Romans 10:17	So faith comes from hearing, and hearing by the word of Christ.
John 8:31-32	So Jesus was saying to those Jews who had believed Him, "If you continue in My word, then you are truly disciples of Mine; and you will know the truth, and the truth will make you free."
Romans 8:2	For the law of the Spirit of life in Christ Jesus has set you free from the law of sin and death.
II Corinthians 2:14	But thanks be to God, who always leads us in triumph in Christ, and manifests through us the sweet aroma of the knowledge of Him in every place.
I John 3:8	The one who practices sin is of the devil; for the devil has sinned from the beginning. The Son of God appeared for this purpose, to destroy the works of the devil.
Philippians 4:6-7	Be anxious for nothing, but in everything by prayer and supplication with thanksgiving let your requests be made known to God. And the peace of God, which surpasses all comprehension, will guard your hearts and your minds in Christ Jesus.
John 14:23	Jesus answered and said to him, "If anyone loves Me, he will keep My word; and My Father will love him, and We will come to him and make our abode with him."
John 15:7-8	"If you abide in Me, and My words abide in you, ask what ever you wish, and it will be done for you. My Father is glorified by this, that you bear much fruit, and so to prove to be My disciples."

Depression

II Samuel 22:17-18   He sent from above, He took me; He drew me out of many waters; He delivered me from my strong enemy, and from them that hated me: for they were too strong for me.

Psalm 18:16-18   He sent from above, He took me, He drew me out of many waters. He delivered me from my strong enemy, and from them which hated me: for they were too strong for me. They prevented me in the day of my calamity: but the LORD was my stay.

Psalm 27:5   For in the time of trouble He shall hide me in His pavilion in the secret of His tabernacle shall He hide me; He shall set me up upon a rock.

Psalm 31:9-14   Have mercy upon me, O LORD, for I am in trouble: mine eye is consumed with grief, yea, my soul and my belly. For my life is spent with grief, and my years with sighing: my strength fails because of my iniquity, and my bones are consumed. I was a reproach among all my enemies, but especially among my neighbors, and a fear to mine acquaintance: they that did see me without, fled from me. I am forgotten as a dead man out of mind: I am like a broken vessel. For I have heard the slander of many: fear was on every side: while they took counsel together against me, they devised to take away my life. But I trusted in thee, O LORD: I said, "Thou art my God."

Psalm 34:17-18   The righteous cry, and the LORD heareth, and delivered them out of all their troubles. The LORD is nigh unto them that are of a broken heart; and saveth such as be of a contrite spirit.

Discouragement and Disappointments

Deuteronomy 31:6,8   Be strong and of a good courage, fear not, nor be afraid of them: for the LORD thy GOD, he it is that doth go with thee; he will not fail thee, nor forsake

	thee. And the LORD, he it is that do go before thee; he will be with thee, he will not fail thee, neither forsake thee: Fear not, neither be dismayed.
Psalms 107:19	Then they cry unto the LORD in their trouble, and he saveth them out of their distresses.
Isaiah 41:10,13	Fear thou not; for I am with thee: be not dismayed; for I am thy God: I will strengthen thee; yea, I will help thee; yea, I will uphold thee with the right hand of my righteousness. For I the LORD thy God will hold thy right hand, saying unto thee, Fear not; I will help thee.
Matthew 6:33	"But seek first His kingdom and His righteousness, and all these things will be added to you."
Matthew 11:28	"Come to me, all who are weary and heavy-laden, and I will give you rest."
I Corinthians 2:9	But just as it is written, "THINGS WHICH EYE HAS NOT SEEN AND EAR HAS NOT HEARD, AND WHICH HAVE NOT ENTERED THE HEART OF MAN, ALL THAT GOD HAS PREPARED FOR THOSE WHO LOVE HIM."
Philippians 1:6	For I am confident of this very thing, that He that began a good work in you will perfect it until the day of Christ Jesus.
Philippians 4:6	Be anxious for nothing, but in everything by prayer and supplication with thanksgiving let your requests be made known to God.
Hebrews 13:5	Make sure that your character is free from the love of money, being content with what you have; for He Himself has said, "I WILL NEVER DESERT YOU, NOR WILL I EVER FORSAKE YOU."

I John 5:4	For whatever is born of God overcomes the world; and this is the victory that has overcome the world—our faith.
Matthew 9:29	Then He touched their eyes, saying, "It shall be done to you according to your faith."
Matthew 15:28	Then Jesus said to her, "O woman, your faith is great; it shall be done for you as you wish." And her daughter was healed at once. (Our will is also involved.)
Matthew 21:21-22	And Jesus answered and said to them, "Truly, I say to you, if you have faith and do not doubt, you will not only do what was done to the fig tree, but even if you say to this mountain, 'Be taken up and cast into the sea,' it will happen. And all things you ask in prayer, believing, you will receive."
Romans 1:16-17	For I am not ashamed of the gospel, for it is the power of God for salvation to everyone who believes, to the Jew first, and also to the Greek. For in it the righteousness of God is revealed from faith to faith; as it is written. "BUT THE RIGHTEOUS *man* SHALL LIVE BY FAITH."
Romans 5:1	Therefore, having been justified by faith, we have peace with God through our Lord Jesus Christ.
Romans 10:8	But what does it say? "THE WORD IS NEAR YOU, IN YOUR MOUTH AND IN YOUR HEART."—that is, the word of faith which we are preaching.
Romans 10:17	So faith comes from hearing, and hearing by the word of Christ.
Galatians 3:23-26	But before faith came, we were kept in custody under the law; being shut up to the faith which was later to be revealed. Therefore, the law has become

	our tutor to lead us to Christ, so that we may be justified by faith. But now that faith has come, we are no longer under a tutor. For you are all children of God through faith in Christ Jesus.
Romans 12:3	For through the grace given to me I say to every one among you not to think more highly of himself than he ought to think; but to think so as to have sound judgment, as God has allotted to each a measure of faith.
I Corinthian 2:3-5	I was with you in weakness and in fear and in much trembling, and my message and my preaching were not in persuasive words of wisdom, but in demonstration of the Spirit and of power, so that your faith would not rest on the wisdom of men, but on the power of God.
Ephesians 2:8-9	For by grace you have been saved through faith; and that not of yourselves, it is the gift of God; not as a result of works, so that no one may boast.
Philemon 6	And I pray that the fellowship of your faith may become effective through the knowledge of every good thing which is in you for Christ's sake.
Hebrews 10:38	BUT MY RIGHTEOUS ONE SHALL LIVE BY FAITH; AND IF HE SHRINKS BACK, MY SOUL HAS NO PLEASURE IN HIM.
Hebrews 11:1	Now faith is the assurance of things hoped for, the conviction of things not seen.
Hebrews 11:6	And without faith it is impossible to please Him, for he who comes to God must believe that He is and that He is a rewarder of those who seek Him.

Faith - Wavering

Luke 9:62	But Jesus said to him, "No one, after putting his hand to the plow and looking back, is fit for the kingdom of God."

John 6:61-69	But Jesus, conscious that His disciples grumbled at this, said to them, "Does this cause you to stumble? What then if you see the Son of Man ascending to where He was before? It is the Spirit who gives life; the flesh profits nothing; the words that I have spoken to you they are spirit and are life. But there are some of you who do not believe." For Jesus knew from the beginning who they were who did not believe and who it was that would betray Him. And He was saying, "For this reason I have said to you, that no one can come to Me unless it has been granted him from the Father." As a result of this many of His disciples withdrew and were not willing to walk with Him anymore. So Jesus said to the twelve, "You do not want to go away also, do you?" Simon Peter answered Him, "Lord, to whom shall we go? You have the words of eternal life. We have believed and have come to know that You are the Holy One of God."
Hebrews 4:14-16	Therefore, since we have a great high priest who has passed through the heavens, Jesus, the Son of God, let us hold fast our confession. For we do not have a high priest who cannot sympathize with our weaknesses, but One who has been tempted in all things as we are, yet without sin. Therefore, let us draw near with confidence to the throne of grace, so that we may receive mercy, and find grace to help in time of need.
Hebrews 10:23	Let us hold fast the confession of our hope without wavering, for He who promises is faithful.
Hebrews 10:38	BUT MY RIGHTEOUS ONE SHALL LIVE BY FAITH; AND IF HE SHRINKS BACK, MY SOUL HAS NO PLEASURE IN HIM.
Hebrews 12:4-6	You have not yet resisted to the point of shedding blood in your striving against sin; and you have forgotten the exhortation which is addressed to you as sons, "MY SON, DO NOT REGARD LIGHTLY THE DISCIPLINE OF THE LORD, NOR FAINT WHEN YOU ARE REPROVED OF HIM;

FOR THOSE WHOM THE LORD LOVES HE DISCIPLINES, AND HE SCOURGES EVERY SON WHOM HE RECEIVES."

Hebrews 12:25   See to it that you do not refuse Him who is speaking. For if those did not escape when they refused him who warned them on earth, much less will we escape from Him who warns from heaven.

Families — For a Closer Walk

Families — Praying for Our Children

Psalms 86:15-16   But thou, O Lord, art a God full of compassion, and gracious, longsuffering, and plenteous in mercy and truth. O turn unto me, and have mercy upon me; give thy strength unto thy servant and save the child of thine handmaid.

Psalms 103:17-18   But the mercy of the LORD is from everlasting to everlasting upon them that fear Him, and His righteousness unto children's children; to such as keep His covenant, and to those that remember His commandments to do them.

Isaiah 44:3-4   For I will pour water upon him that is thirsty, and floods upon dry ground: I will pour my spirit upon thy seed, and my blessing upon thy offspring: and they shall spring up as among the grass, as will willows by the water courses.

Isaiah 54:13   And all thy children shall be taught of the LORD; and great shall be the peace of thy children.

Isaiah 59:21   As for me, this is my covenant with them, saith the LORD; My Spirit that is upon thee, and my words that I have put in thy mouth, shall not depart out of thy mouth, nor out of the mouth of thy seed, nor out of the mouth of thy seed's seed, saith the LORD, from henceforth and forever.

Acts 16:31-32	They said, "Believe in the Lord Jesus, and you will be saved, you and your household." And they spoke the word of the Lord to him, together with all who were in his house.
Ephesians 5:15-17	Therefore be careful how you walk, not as unwise men but as wise, making the most of your time, because the days are evil. So then do not be foolish, but understand what the will of the Lord is.
Ephesians 6:1-4	Children, obey your parents in the Lord, for this is right. HONOR YOUR FATHER AND MOTHER (Which is the first commandment with a promise), SO THAT IT MAY BE WELL WITH YOU, AND THAT YOU MAY LIVE LONG ON THE EARTH. Fathers, do not provoke your children to anger, but bring them up in the discipline and instruction of the Lord.
II Peter 3:8-9	But do not let this one fact escape your notice, beloved, that with the Lord, one day is like a thousand years, and a thousand years as one day. The Lord is not slow about His promise, as some count slowness, but is patient toward you, not wishing for any to perish but for all to come to repentance.

(Children who have been dedicated to the Lord, and then become bound in sin, still belong to God.)

Philippians 1:6	For I am confident of this very thing, that He who began a good work in you will perfect it until the day of Christ Jesus.
I Peter 1:3-6	Blessed be the God and Father of our Lord Jesus Christ, who according to His great mercy has caused us to be born again to a living hope through the resurrection of Jesus Christ from the dead, to obtain an inheritance which is imperishable and undefiled and will not fade away, reserved in heaven for you, who are protected by the power of God through faith for

a salvation ready to be revealed in the last time. In this you greatly rejoice, even though now for a little while, if necessary, you have been distressed by various trials.

Hebrews 1:13-14 But to which of the angels has He ever said, "SIT AT MY RIGHT HAND, UNTIL I MAKE YOUR ENEMIES A FOOTSTOOL FOR YOUR FEET?" Are they not all ministering spirits, sent out to render service for the sake of those who will inherit salvation?

(We pray for angelic protection for our children)

John 10:27-28 "My sheep hear My voice, and I know them, and they follow Me; and I will give eternal live to them, and they will never perish, and no one will snatch them out of My hand."

I Thessalonians 5:23-24

Now may the God of peace Himself sanctify you entirely; and may your spirit and soul and body be preserved complete, without blame at the coming of our Lord Jesus Christ. Faithful is He who calls you, and He also will bring it to pass.

As you look at your child's ungodly ways, it may cause you to bring them into a bondage of judgment. Start trusting God and His word. His promises are sure! We free God's hands to work in their lives as we forgive them, love them, and pray God's promises to turn them from their ungodly behavior.

They also need to learn about God's grace, mercy and forgiveness through their life experiences. Your belief and trust in God's word in your life when observed by them, will draw them more quickly into submission to the Lord's will. (Matthew 12:37; Romans 2:1; and Proverbs 18:21)

Children Involved in False Religions and Doctrines of Devils, Superstitions, Idolatry, Divination and Magic, Humanism, and Atheism.

Parents, pray and claim by faith that your children be born again and delivered from the curse of the law. Claim the following verse for them.

Galatians 3:13-14   Christ redeemed us from the curse of the law, having become a curse for us – for it is written, "CURSED IS EVERYONE WHO HANGS ON A TREE" – in order that in Christ Jesus the blessing of Abraham might come to the Gentiles, so that we would receive the promise of the Spirit through faith.

Because they are the seed of the righteous, you, as a believer in Christ Jesus, may pray the above promise for your children.

Now, pray the following for your children:

In the name of Jesus, I bind the unclean spirits now in my child:

Name_____
I ask you Lord to fill_____with your Holy Spirit and the spirits of love, joy, peace, healing, truth etc.
Lord God I especially pray your scripture promises in:_____
_____, use specific verses and recite the promise.
Thank you Lord God for honoring your Word.
Then give praise to God for hearing and answering your prayer.

Farmers Provisions

Job 39:12   Do you have faith in him that he will return, and bring your grain to your threshing floor?

Psalms 67:5-7   Let the people praise thee O God;
let all the people praise thee. Then
shall the earth yield her increase; and
God, even our God, shall bless us.
God shall bless us; and all the ends
of the earth shall fear him

Proverbs 3:9-10   Honor the Lord with your substance,
And with the first fruits of all your produce;
Then your barns will be filled with plenty,
Your vats will be bursting with wine.

Proverbs 6:6-11	Go to the ant, thou sluggard; consider her ways, and be wise: which having no guide, overseer, or ruler, provideth her meat in the summer, and gathereth her food in the harvest. How long wilt thou sleep, O sluggard? When wilt thou rise out of thy sleep? Yet a little sleep, a little slumber, a little folding of the hands to sleep: So shall thy poverty come as one that travelleth, and thy want as an armed man.
Proverbs 10:5	He that gathereth in summer is a wise son: but he that sleepeth in harvest is a son that causeth shame.
Proverbs 12:11	He that tilleth his land shall be satisfied with bread: but he that followeth vain persons is void of understanding.
Proverbs 20:4	The sluggard will not plow by reason of the cold; therefore shall he beg in harvest and have nothing.
Proverbs 24:27	Prepare thy work without, and make it fit for thyself in the field; afterwards build thy house.
Proverbs 27:23	Be thou diligent to know the state of thy flocks, and look well to thy herds.

Fasting

(From early in scriptures, we have been called to fast.)

Exodus 34:28	And he was there with the Lord forty days and forty nights; he did neither eat bread, nor drink water. And he wrote upon the tables the words of the covenant, the ten commandments.
Leviticus 23:26-28	And the LORD spake unto Moses, saying, Also on the tenth day of this seventh month there shall be a day of atonement: it shall be an holy convocation unto you; and ye shall afflict your souls, and offer an offering made by fire unto the LORD.

Ezra 8:21-23   Then I proclaimed a fast there, at the river of A-hava, that we might afflict ourselves before our God, to seek of Him a right way for us, and for our little ones, and for all our substance. For I was ashamed to require of the king a band of soldiers and horsemen to help us against the enemy in the way: because we had spoken unto the king, saying, the hand of our God is upon all them for good that seek him; but his power and his wrath is against all them that forsake him. So we fasted and besought our God for this: and he was intreated of us.

Nehemiah 1:4   And it came to pass, when I heard these words, that I sat down and wept, and mourned certain days, and fasted, and prayed before the God of heaven.

Nehemiah 9:1   Now in the twenty and fourth day of this month the children of Israel were assembled with fasting, and with sackclothes, and with earth upon them.

Isaiah 58:6-11   Is this not the fast that I have chosen? To loosen the bands of wickedness, to undo the heavy burdens, and to let the oppressed go free, and that ye break every yoke? Is it not to deal thy bread to the hungry and that thou bring the poor that are cast out to thy house? When thou seest the naked, that thou cover him; and that thou hide not thyself from thine own flesh? Then shall thy light break forth like the morning, and thine health shall spring forth speedily: and thy righteousness shall go before thee; the glory of the LORD shall be thy rereward. (rear guard) Then shalt thou call, and the LORD shall answer; thou shalt cry, and he shall say, Here I am. If thou take away from the midst of thee the yoke, the putting forth of the finger, and speaking vanity; and if thou draw out thy soul to the hungry, and satisfy the afflicted soul; then shall thy light rise in obscurity, and thy darkness shall be as the noon day. And the LORD shall guide thee continually, and satisfy thy soul in drought, and make fat thy bones: and thou shalt be like a watered garden, and like a spring of water, whose waters fail not.

Joel 2:12

Yet even now, says the Lord,
"Return to me with all your heart, with fasting, with weeping, and with mourning."

Matthew 6:16-18

"Whenever you fast, do not put on a gloomy face, as the hypocrites do, for they neglect their appearance so they will be noticed by men when they are fasting. Truly, I say to you, they have their reward in full. But you, when you fast, anoint your head and wash your face, so that your fasting will not be noticed by men, but by your Father who is in secret; and your Father who sees what is done in secret will reward you."

Luke 4:1-2

Jesus, full of the Holy Spirit, returned from the Jordan, and was led around by the Spirit in the wilderness for forty days, being tempted by the devil. And He ate nothing during those days, and when they had ended, He became hungry.

Acts 13:2-3

While they were ministering to the Lord and fasting, the Holy Spirit said, "Set apart for Me Barnabas and Saul for the work to which I have called them." Then when they had fasted and prayed and laid their hands on them, they sent them away.

Acts 14:23

When they had appointed elders for them in every church, having prayed with fasting, they commended them to the Lord in whom they had believed.

I Corinthians 7:5

Stop depriving one another, except by agreement for a time, so that Satan will not tempt you because of your lack of self-control; so that you may devote yourselves to prayer, and come together again.

Fear

Fear is from Satan. This is one of the strong ways in which he tries to control humankind. The Sword of the Spirit spoken in faith out loud will destroy this "strongman" of the devil when applied. Say it often until your mind and heart is full of God's peace and fear is gone! In Mark 11:23, the word "says" in Greek means, continuous action, continuously saying!

Deuteronomy 31:8	And the LORD, he it is that doth go before thee; he will be with thee, he will not fail thee, neither forsake thee: fear not, neither be dismayed.
Psalms 23:4	Yea, thou I walk through the valley of the shadow of death, I will fear no evil: for thou art with me; thy rod and thy staff they comfort me.
Psalms 34:4	I sought the LORD, and he heard me, and delivered me from all my fears.
Psalms 91:5	Thou shalt not be afraid for the terror by night; nor for the arrow that flieth by day.
Proverbs 18:10	The name of the LORD is a strong tower: the righteous runneth into it, and is safe.
Isaiah 41:10	Fear thou not; for I am with thee: be not dismayed; for I am thy God: I will strengthen thee; yea, I will help thee; yea, I will uphold thee with the right hand of my righteousness.
Matthew 28:	Teach them to observe all that I have commanded you; and lo, I am with you always, even unto the end of the age.
Luke 12:7	"Indeed, the very hairs of your head are numbered. Do not fear; you are more valuable than many sparrows."
Romans 8:15	For you have not received a spirit of slavery leading to fear again, but you have received a spirit of adoption as sons by which we cry out, "Abba! Father!"

II Thessalonians 3:3	But the Lord is faithful, and He will strengthen and protect you from the evil one.
II Timothy 1:7	For God has not given us a spirit of timidity, but of power and love and discipline.
I John 4:18	There is no fear in love; but perfect love casts out fear, because fear involves punishment, and the one who fears is not perfected in love.
Revelation 21:6-8	Then He said to me, "It is done. I am the Alpha and the Omega, the beginning and the end. I will give to the one who thirsts from the spring of water of life without cost. He who overcomes will inherit these things, and I will be his God and he will be my son. But for the cowardly and unbelieving and abominable and murderers and immoral persons and sorcerers and idolaters and all liars, their part will be in the lake that burns with fire and brimstone, which is the second death."

MEDITATIONS
Sts. Timothy and Titus
2 Timothy 1:1-8

God did not give us a spirit of timidity, but of power and love and discipline. (2 Timothy 1:7)

    Paul told Timothy--a somewhat timid apostle--to fan the flame of the Spirit within him so that he could be more effective in leading the church in Ephesus. Yet Paul's command was not only for this one man in a particularly challenging situation. These words apply just as much to us, whatever our situations! After all, the same Spirit that raised Christ from the dead--the same Spirit that empowered Timothy--lives in us as well!
    Why should we fan the flame of the Spirit? Because God wants us to make a difference in this world, and He knows that we cannot do this on our own strength. Only Christ in us, the hope of glory, can empower us to build the kingdom of God. At the same time, we can't just sit around and expect God to do the work in us, for faith without action is dead (James

2:17). No, we must step out in faith, learning to rely on the spiritual gifts Jesus has given us.

So what practical steps can we take? How can we actually "fan the flame?" If we begin by following Jesus in the small things, not only will our faith grow but so will our experience of God's power. Maybe that means establishing a time once a week to pray with our children. Maybe it means setting aside a part of our finances to help the poor and needy.

Maybe it means doing something extra for our spouse to demonstrate our love. The possibilities are endless, and all of them can become a way to fan the flame if we ask the Holy Spirit to bless them.

> "Ascribe to the Lord the
> glory of His name!"
> —Psalms 96:8

This is probably how Timothy and Titus became so effective as apostles, bishops, and witnesses to the resurrection. Like the rest of us, they each had their own strengths and weaknesses. But over time, as they cooperated with the Holy Spirit, they both saw God work wonders in them and through them.

> "Lord, thank you for the gift of
> your Spirit. Help me to move in this
> world with greater confidence in you.
> Jesus, I want to be your servant."

Psalms 96:1-3, 7-8, 10; Mark 3:22-30 - January 2004
Reprinted with permission of "The Word Among Us"
9639 Dr Perry Rd #126
Ijamsville, MD 21754
Issue Date January 2004

The "Word Among Us" is a valuable source of encouragement for meditation of the sacred scriptures. For a subscription they can be reached at: 1-800-775-9673
- Joseph & Ruth Wesley

Fear of Man

Psalms 56:11-12
In God have I put my trust: I will not be afraid what man can do unto me. Thy vows are upon me, O God: I will render praises unto thee.

Proverbs 29:25
The fear of man bringeth a snare: but who so putteth his trust in the LORD shall be safe.

Isaiah 51:7
Hearken unto me, ye that know righteousness, the people in whose heart is my law; fear ye not the reproach of men, neither be ye afraid of their revilings.

Hebrews 13:5-6
Make sure that your character is free from the love of money, being content with what you have; for He Himself has said, "I WILL NEVER DESERT YOU, NOR WILL I EVER FORSAKE YOU," so that we confidently say, "THE LORD IS MY HELPER, I WILL NOT BE AFRAID. WHAT WILL MAN DO TO ME?"

Fear of the Lord

IT IS NOT;
Natural Fear: For a person's protection or
Demonic Fear: That torments and enslaves.

II Timothy 1:7
For God has not given us a spirit of timidity, but of power and love and discipline.

I John 4:18
There is no fear in love; but perfect love casts out fear, because fear involves punishment, and the one who fears is not perfected in love.

Fear of man:

Isaiah 51:7,12
Hearken unto me, ye that know righteousness, the people in whose heart is my law; fear ye not the reproach of men, neither be ye afraid of their revilings. I, even I, am he that comforts you; who art thou, that thou should be afraid of a man that shall die and of the son of man which shall be made as grass.

Proverbs 29:25	The fear of man bringeth a snare: but whoso putteth his trust in the LORD shall be safe.
Psalms 56:11	In God I have put my trust; I will not be afraid what man can do unto me.
Colossians 3:16-17	Let the word of Christ dwell richly within you, with all wisdom teaching and admonishing one another with psalms and hymns and spiritual songs, singing with thankfulness in your hearts to God. Whatever you do in word or deed, do all in the name of the Lord Jesus, giving thanks through Him to God the Father.
IT IS:	**Fear of the Lord** is an awe of God, a reverence for God, a listening to God with an open heart that seeks to understand Him and will love Him and obey Him.
Deuteronomy 5:29	O that there were such an heart in them, that they would fear me, and keep my commandments always, that it may be well with them, and with their children.
Psalms 25:12-14	What man is he that feareth the LORD? Him shall he teach in the way that he shall choose. His soul shall dwell at ease; and his seed shall inherit the earth. The secret of the LORD is with them that fear him; and he will shew them in His covenant.
Psalms 19:8-9	The statutes of the LORD are right, rejoicing the heart: the commandment of the LORD is pure, enlightening the eyes. The fear of the LORD is clean, enduring for ever: the judgments of the LORD are true and righteous altogether.
Psalms 31:19-20	O how great is the goodness which thou hast laid up for them that fear thee; which thou hast wrought for them that trust in thee before the sons of men!

	Thou shalt hide them in the secret of thy presence from the pride of man: thou shalt keep them secretly in a pavilion from the strife of tongues.
Psalms 33:18-22	Behold, the eye of the LORD is upon them that fear him, upon them that hope in his mercy; to deliver their soul from death, and to keep them alive in famine. Our soul waiteth for the LORD: he is our help and our shield. For our heart shall rejoice in him, because we have trusted in his holy name. Let thy mercy, O LORD, be upon us, according as we hope in thee.
Psalms 34:7-10	The angel of the LORD encampeth round about them that fear him, and delivereth them. O taste and see that the LORD is good: blessed is the man that trusteth in him. O fear the LORD, ye his saints: for there is no want to them that fear him. The young lions do lack, and suffer hunger: but they that seek the LORD shall not want any good thing.
Psalms 111:10	The fear of the LORD is the beginning of wisdom: a good understanding have all they that do his commandments: his praise endureth for ever.
Psalms 145:19	He will fulfill the desire of them that fear him: he will also hear their cry, and will save them.
Psalms 147:11	The LORD taketh pleasure in them that fear him, in those who hope in his mercy.
Proverbs 2:1-5	My son, if thou wilt receive my words, and hide my commandments with thee; so that thou incline thine ear unto wisdom, and apply thine heart to understanding; yea, if thou criest after knowledge, and liftest up thy voice for understanding; if thou seekest her as silver, and searchest for her as for hid treasures; then shalt thou understand the fear of the LORD and find the knowledge of God.

Proverbs 14:26	In the fear of the LORD is strong confidence: and his children shall have a place of refuge.
Proverbs 15:33	The fear of the LORD is the instruction of wisdom; and before honor is humility.
Malachi 3:16-18	Then they that feared the LORD spake often one to another: and the LORD hearkened, and heard it, and a book of remembrance was written before him for them that fear the LORD, and that thought upon his name.
Malachi 4:2	But unto you that fear my name shall the Sun of Righteousness arise with healing in his wings; and ye shall go forth, and grow up as calves of the stall.

Forgiveness

One who will not forgive forms a root of bitterness.

Isaiah 55:7	Let the wicked forsake his way, and the unrighteous man, his thoughts: and let him return unto the LORD, and he will have mercy upon him; and to our God, for he will abundantly pardon.
Matthew 5:23-24	"Therefore if you are presenting your offering at the altar, and there remember that your brother has something against you, leave your offering there before the altar and go; first be reconciled to your brother, and then come and present your offering.
Matthew 6:14-15	"For if you forgive others for their transgressions, your heavenly Father will also forgive you. But if you do not forgive others, then your Father will not forgive your transgressions."
Matthew 18:35	"My heavenly Father will also do the same to you, if each of you does not forgive his brother from your heart."

Mark 11:25	"Whenever you stand praying, forgive, if you have anything against anyone, so that your Father who is in heaven will also forgive you your transgressions."
Romans 12:14	Bless those who persecute you; bless and do not curse.
John 3:16-17	"For God so loved the world, that He gave His only begotten Son, that whoever believes in Him shall not perish, but have eternal life. For God did not send His Son into the world to judge the world, but that the world might be saved through Him."

(We are all already condemned because of our sins. A belief, trust, surrender to Jesus as Lord, through repentance and a prayer of faith, is the only way to be saved. Our good works will be the result of being saved!)

Colossians 3:12-13	So, as those who have been chosen of God, holy and beloved, put on a heart of compassion, kindness, humility, gentleness, and patience; bearing with one another and forgiving each other, whoever has a complaint against anyone, just as the Lord forgave you, so also should you.
Ephesians 4:31-32	Let all bitterness and wrath and anger and clamor and slander be put away from you, along with malice. Be kind to one another, tender-hearted, compassionate, forgiving each other, just as God in Christ also has forgiven you.
	Beam out forgiveness to those who have harmed or hurt you. Ask God to forgive them, and have mercy upon them, in a unilateral declaration, just as Jesus said on the Cross. The reconciling power of the cross will bring about miracles in that very hour.
Isaiah 53:5, I Corinthians 5:18-20, Colossians 1:20	
	This peace speaks about rest, health, and wholeness because relationships are at peace.

Matthew 12:34	"For the mouth speaks out of that which fills the heart."
	When it is hard to forgive, your confession shows what is in your heart. (You still resent what someone did.) Do as Jesus did in Luke 23:34, and say, "Father, forgive them, for they know not what they do." An unforgiving heart robs one of all the blessings of the Lord, as well as health and answers to prayer. Why? You placed these people in the bondage of judgment through your words of condemnation when they originally hurt, offended, harmed, or cheated you.
II Peter 3:9	The Lord is not slow about his promise as some count slowness, but is forbearing toward you, not wishing that any should perish, but that all should reach repentance.

God's Presence

Exodus 14:19	And the angel of God, which went before the camp of Israel, removed and went behind them; and the pillar of the cloud went from before their face, and stood behind them.
Exodus 33:14	And he said, my presence shall go with thee, and I will give thee rest.
Deuteronomy 4:39	Know therefore this day, and consider it in thine heart, that the LORD he is God in heaven above, and upon earth beneath; there is no one else.
Psalms 5:11-12	But let all those that put their trust in thee rejoice: let them ever shout for joy, because thou defendest them: let them also that love thy name be joyful in thee. For thou, LORD, wilt bless the righteous; with favor wilt thou compass him as with a shield.
Psalms 16:8	I have set the LORD always before me: because he is my right hand, I shall not be moved.

Psalms 125:2	As the mountains are round about Jerusalem, so the LORD is round about his people from henceforth even forever.
Isaiah 52:12	For ye shall not go out with haste, nor go by flight: for the LORD will go before you; and the God of Israel will be your rereward (rear guard).
Ezekiel 36:27	And I will put my Spirit within you, and cause you to walk in my statutes, and ye shall keep my judgments, and do them.
Matthew 28:20	Teaching them to observe all that I commanded you; and I am with you always, even to the end of the age.

Guidance and Direction

Deuteronomy 31:6	Be strong and of a good courage, fear not, nor be afraid of them: for the LORD thy God, he it is that doth go with thee; he will not fail thee nor forsake thee.
Psalms 16:11	Thou wilt shew me the path of life: in thy presence is fullness of joy; at thy right hand there are pleasures for evermore.
Psalms 25:8-9	Good and upright is the LORD: therefore he will teach sinners in the way. The meek he will guide in judgment: and the meek will he teach his way.
Psalms 31:2-3	Bow down thy ear to me; deliver me speedily: be thou my strong rock, for an house of defense to save me. For thou art my rock and fortress: therefore for thy names sake, lead me, and guide me.
Psalms 32:8	I will instruct and teach thee in the way that you should go: I will guide thee with mine eye.
Psalms 37:23	The steps of a good man are ordered of the LORD: and he delighteth in his way.

Psalms 58:10	The righteous shall rejoice when he seeth the vengeance: he shall wash his feet in the blood of the wicked.
Psalms 73:23	Nevertheless I am continually with thee; thou hast holden me by my right hand.
Psalms 78:72	So he fed them according to the integrity of his heart; and guided them with the skillfulness of his hands.
Psalms 119:105	Thy word is a lamp unto my feet and a light unto my path.
Psalms 119:133	Order my steps in thy word: and let not any iniquity have dominion over me.
Psalms 121:8	The LORD shall preserve thy going out and thy coming in from this time forth, and even for evermore.
Proverbs 2:8	He keepeth the paths of judgment, and preserveth the way of his saints.
Proverbs 3:5-6	Trust in the LORD with all thine heart; and lean not unto thine own understanding. In all thy ways acknowledge him, and he shall direct thy paths.
Proverbs 11:3	The integrity of the upright shall guide them: but the perverseness of transgressors shall destroy them.
Isaiah 30:21	And thine ear shall hear a word behind thee, saying, This is the way, walk ye in it, when ye turn to the right hand, and when ye turn to the left.
Isaiah 45:2	I will go before thee, and make the crooked places straight: I will break in pieces the gates of brass, and cut in sunder the bars of iron.
Luke 1:79	TO SHINE UPON THOSE WHO SIT IN DARKNESS AND THE SHADOW OF DEATH, To guide our feet into the way of peace.

Luke 21:15	For I will give you utterance and wisdom none of your opponents will be able to resist or refute.
John 14:26	"But the Helper, the Holy Spirit, whom the Father will send in My name, He will teach you all things, and bring to your remembrance all that I said to you."
John 16:13	"But when He, the Spirit of truth, comes, He will guide you into the truth; for He will not speak on His own initiative, but whatever He hears, He will speak; and He will disclose to you what is to come."
Revelation 3:8	'I know your deeds. Behold, I have put before you an open door which no one can shut, because you have a little power, and have kept My word, and have not denied My name.'

Healing Scriptures for All Needs

Exodus 23:25	And ye shall serve the LORD your God, and he shall bless thy bread, and thy water; and I will take sickness away from the midst of thee.
Psalms 30:2	O LORD my God, I cried unto thee, and thou hast healed me.
Psalms 34:9	O fear the LORD, ye his saints: for there is no want to them that fear him.
Psalms 55:18	He hath delivered my soul in peace, from the battle that was against me: for there were many (against) with me.
Psalms 97:10	Ye that love the LORD hate evil: he preserveth the souls of his saints; he delivereth them out of the hand of the wicked.
Psalms 103:2-3	Bless the LORD, O my soul, and forget not all his benefits: Who forgiveth all thine iniquities; who healeth all thy diseases.

Psalms 119:93	I will never forget thy precepts: for with them thou hast quickened me.
Isaiah 53:4-5	Surely he hath born our grief, and carried our sorrows: yet we did esteem him stricken, smitten of God, and afflicted. But he was wounded for our transgressions, he was bruised for our iniquities: the chastisement of our peace was upon him; and with his stripes we are healed.
Isaiah 58:8	Than shall thy light break forth as the morning, and thine health shall spring forth speedily: and thy righteousness shall go before thee; the glory of the LORD shall be thy rereward.(rearguard)
Matthew 8:17	This was to fulfill what was spoken through Isaiah the prophet: "HE HIMSELF TOOK OUR INFIRMITIES AND CARRIED AWAY OUR DISEASES."
Romans 8:2	For the law of the Spirit of life in Christ Jesus has set you free from the law of sin and of death.
Romans 8:11	But if the Spirit of Him who raised Jesus from the dead dwells in you, He who raised Christ from the dead will also give life to your mortal bodies through His Spirit who dwells in you.
Romans 8:32	He who did not spare His own Son, but delivered Him over for us all, how will He not also with Him freely give us all things?
II Corinthians 2:14	But thanks be to God, who always leads us in triumph in Christ, and manifests to us the sweet aroma of the knowledge of Him in every place.
III John 2	Beloved, I pray that in all respects you may prosper and be in good health, just as your soul prospers.

I Peter 2:24	And He Himself bore our sins in His body on the cross, so that we might die to sin and live in righteousness; for by His wounds you were healed.

Healing Scriptures

Abdomen

Psalms 30:2	O LORD my God, I cried unto thee, and thou hast healed me.
Proverbs 3:7-8	Be not wise in thine own eyes, fear the LORD, and depart from evil. It shall be health to thy navel, and marrow to thy bones.
Proverbs 4:20-22	My son, attend to my words; incline thine ear unto my sayings. Let them not depart from thine eyes; keep them in the midst of thine heart. For they are life to all those that find them, and health to all their flesh.

Allergy-Sinus

Psalms 25:17-18	The troubles of my heart are enlarged: O bring thou me out of my distresses. Look upon mine affliction and my pain; and forgive all my sins.
Psalms 32:6	For this shall everyone that is godly pray unto thee in a time when thou mayest be found: surely in the floods of great waters they shall not come nigh unto him.
Psalms 42:11	Why art thou cast down, O my soul? and why art thou disquieted within me? hope thou in God: for I shall yet praise Him, who is the health of my countenance and my God.
Psalms 69:15	Let not the water-flood overflow me, neither let the deep swallow me up, and let not the pit shut her mouth upon me.

Psalms 144:7-8	Send thine hand from above; rid me, and deliver me out of great waters, from the hand of strange children; Whose mouth speaketh vanity, and their right hand is a right hand of falsehood.

Arthritis

Job 4:3-4	Behold, thou hast instructed many, and thou hast strengthened the weak hands. Thy words have upholden him that was falling, and thou hast strengthened the feeble knees.
Psalms 145:14	The LORD upholdeth all that fall, and raiseth up all those that be bowed down.
Psalms 146:5-8	Happy is he that hath the God of Jacob for his help, whose hope is in the LORD his God: Which made heaven, and earth, the sea, and all that therein is: which keepeth truth forever: Which executeth judgment for the oppressed: which giveth food to the hungry. The LORD looseth the prisoners: the LORD openeth the eyes of the blind: the LORD raiseth them that are bowed down: the LORD loveth the righteous.
Proverbs 14:30	A sound heart is the life of the flesh: but envy the rottenness of the bones.
Proverbs 16:24	Pleasant words are as an honeycomb, sweet to the soul and health to the bones.
Isaiah 35:3	Strengthen ye the weak hands, and confirm the feeble knees.
Hebrews 12:12-13	Therefore, strengthen the hands that are weak and the knees that are feeble, and make straight paths for your feet, so that the limb that is lame may not be put out of joint, but rather be healed.

Asthma

Psalms 91:3-4 — Surely he shall deliver thee from the snare of the fowler, and from the noisome pestilence. He shall cover thee with his feathers, and under his wings shalt thou trust: his truth shall be thy shield and buckler.

Lamentations 3:56 — Thou hast heard my voice: hide not thine ear at my breathing, at my cry.

Joel 2:32 — And it shall come to pass, that whosoever shall call on the name of the LORD shall be delivered: for in mount Zion and in Jerusalem shall be deliverance, as the LORD hath said, and in the remnant whom the LORD shall call.

Acts 17:25 — Nor is He served by human hands, as though He needed anything, since He Himself gives to all people life and breath and all things.

Barrenness

Genesis 18:14 — Is anything too hard for the LORD? At the time appointed I will return unto thee, according to the time of life, and Sarah shall have a son.

Deuteronomy 7:9-14 — Know therefore that the LORD thy God, he is God, the faithful God, which keepeth covenant and mercy with them that love him and keep his commandments to a thousand generations; And repayeth them that hate him to their face, to destroy them: he will not be slack to him that hateth him, he will repay him to his face. Thou shalt therefore keep the commandments, and the statutes, and the judgments, which I command thee this day, to do them. Wherefore it shall come to pass, if you have hearken to these judgments, and keep and do them, that the LORD thy God shall keep unto thee the covenant and the mercy which He swore unto thy fathers:

And He will love thee, and bless thee, and multiply thee: he will also bless the fruit of thy womb, and the fruit of thy land, thy corn, and thy wine, and thy oil, the increase of thy kine, and the flocks of thy sheep in the land which He swore unto thy fathers to give thee. Thou shalt be blessed above all people: there shalt not be male or female barren among you, or among your cattle.

Psalms 113:9   He maketh the barren woman to keep house, and to be a joyful mother of children. Praise ye the LORD.

Blood and Diseases of the Blood

Anemia, Blood Pressure, Leukemia, Diabetes

Psalms 138:7   Though I walk in the midst of trouble, thou wilt revive me: and shalt stretch forth thine hand against the wrath of mine ememies, and thy right hand shall save me.

Proverbs 3:5-8   Trust in the LORD with all thine heart; and lean not unto thine own understanding. In all thy ways acknowledge him, and he shall direct thy paths. Be not wise in thine own eyes: fear the LORD, and depart from evil. It shall be health to thy navel, and marrow to thy bones

I Corinthians 3:16   Do you not know that you are a temple of God and that the Spirit of God dwells in you?

Hebrews 4:12   For the word of God is living and active and sharper than any two-edged sword, and piercing as far as the division of soul and spirit, of both joints and marrow, and able to judge the thoughts and intentions of the heart.

Bedwetting

Malachi 4:2   But unto you that fear my name shall the Sun of Righteousness arise with healing in his wings; and ye shall go forth and grow up as calves of the stall.

Psalms 32:6	For this shall every one that is godly pray unto thee in a time when thou mayest be found: surely in floods of great waters they shall not come nigh unto him.
Psalms 69:16-19	Hear me, O LORD; for thy loving kindness is good: turn unto me according to the multitude of thy mercies. Thou hast known my reproach, and my shame, and my dishonor: mine adversaries are all before thee.
Matthew 8:17	This was to fulfill what was spoken through Isaiah the prophet: "HE HIMSELF TOOK OUR INFIRMITIES AND CARRIED AWAY OUR DISEASES."

Bones

Psalms 6:2	Have mercy upon me, O Lord; for I am weak: O Lord, heal me, for my bones are vexed.
Psalms 32: 3-7	When I kept silence, my bones waxed old through my roaring all the day long. For day and night thy hand was heavy upon me: my moisture is turned into the drought of summer. Selah. I acknowledge my sin unto thee, and mine iniquity have I not hid. I said, I will confess my transgressions unto the LORD; and thou forgavest the iniquity of my sin. Selah. For this shall every one that is godly pray unto thee in a time when thou mayest be found: surely in the floods of great waters they shall not come nigh unto him. Thou art my hiding place; thou shalt preserve me from trouble; thou shalt compass me about with songs of deliverance. Selah.
Psalms 34:19-20	Many are the afflictions of the righteous: but the LORD delivereth him out of them all. He keepeth all his bones: not one of them is broken.

Proverbs 3:5-8	Trust in the LORD with all thine heart; and lean not unto thine own understanding. In all thy ways acknowledge him, and he shall direct thy paths. Be not wise in thine own eyes: fear the LORD, and depart from evil. It shall be health to thy navel, and marrow to thy bones.
Isaiah 58:11	And the LORD shall guide thee continually, and satisfy thy soul in drought, and make fat thy bones: and thou shalt be like a watered garden, and like a spring of water whose waters fail not.
Hebrews 4:12	For the word of God is living and active and sharper than any two-edged sword, and piercing as far as the division of soul and spirit, of both joints and marrow, and able to judge the thoughts and intentions of the heart.

Burns and Sunburn

Psalms 121:5-6	The LORD is thy keeper: the LORD is thy shade on thy right hand. The sun shall not smite thee by day, nor the moon by night.
Isaiah 43:2	When you passest through the waters, I will be with thee; and through the rivers, they shall not overflow thee: when thou walkest through the fire, thou shalt not be burned; neither shall the flame kindle upon thee.
Isaiah 49:10	They shall not hunger nor thirst; neither shall the heat nor sun smite them: for he that hath mercy on them shall lead them, even by the springs of water shall he guide them.

Cancer

Proverbs 4:20-22	My son, attend to my words; incline thine ear unto my sayings. Let them not depart from thine eyes; keep them in the midst of thine heart. For they are life unto those that find them, and health to all their flesh.

II Timothy 1:7	For God has not given us a spirit of timidity, but of power and love and discipline.
II Thessalonians 3:3	But the Lord is faithful, and He will strengthen and protect you from the evil one.
Matthew 15:13	But He answered and said, "Every plant which My heavenly Father did not plant shall be uprooted."
Mark 11:24	"Therefore I say to you, all things for which you pray and ask, believe that you have received them, and they will be granted you."

Childbirth

Psalms 91:9-10	Because thou hast made the LORD, which is my refuge, even the most High, thy habitation; there shall no evil befall thee, neither shall any plague come nigh thy dwelling.
Isaiah 66:7	Before she travailed, she brought forth; before her pain came, she was delivered of a man child.
John 16:21	"Whenever a woman is in labor she has pain, because her hour has come; but when she gives birth to the child, she no longer remembers the anguish because of the joy that a child has been brought into the world."
I Timothy 2:15	But women will be preserved through the bearing of children if they continue in faith and love and sanctity with self-restraint.

Colds

Psalms 42:11	Why art thou cast down, O my soul? And why art thou disquieted within me? Hope thou in God: for I shall yet praise him who is the health of my countenance, and my God.

Psalms 91:3	Surely He shall deliver thee from the snare of the fowler, and from the noisome pestilence.

Diseases

Psalms 103:2-3	Bless the LORD, O my soul, and forget not all his benefits: Who forgiveth all thy iniquities; who healeth all thy diseases.
Psalms 107:20	He sent his word, and healed them, and delivered them from their destructions.
Psalms 138	I will praise thee with my whole heart: before the gods will I sing praise unto thee. I will worship toward thy holy temple, and praise thy name for thy loving kindness and for thy truth: for thou hast magnified thy word above all thy name. In the day when I cried thou answeredst me, and strengthenedst me with strength in my soul. All the kings of the earth shall praise thee, O LORD, when they hear the words of thy mouth. Yea, they shall sing in the ways of the LORD: for great is the glory of the LORD. Though the LORD be high, yet hath He respect unto the lowly: but the proud He knoweth afar off. Though I walk in the midst of trouble, thou wilt revive me: thou shalt stretch forth thine hand against the wrath of mine enemies, and thy right hand shall save me. The LORD will perfect that which concerneth me: Thy mercy, O LORD, endureth for ever: forsake not the works of thine own hands.
Proverbs 12:18	There is that speaketh like the piercing of a sword: but the tongue of the wise is health.
Jeremiah 17:14	Heal me, O LORD, and I shall be healed; save me, and I shall be saved: for thou art my praise.
Jeremiah 33:6	Behold, I will bring it health and cure, and I will

	cure them, and will reveal unto them the abundance of peace and truth.
James 5:16	Therefore, confess your sins to one another, and pray for one another so that you may be healed. The effective prayer of a righteous man can accomplish much.
I Peter 3:12	"FOR THE EYES OF THE LORD ARE TOWARD THE RIGHTEOUS, AND HIS EARS ATTEND TO THEIR PRAYER, BUT THE FACE OF THE LORD IS AGAINST THOSE WHO DO EVIL."
III John 2	Beloved, I pray that in all respects you may prosper and be in good health, just as your soul prospers.

Drowning

Psalms 66:6	He turned the sea into dry land: they went through the flood on foot: there did we rejoice in him.
Psalms 107:28-30	Then they cry unto the LORD in their trouble, and he bringeth them out of their distresses. He maketh the storm a calm, so that the waves thereof are still. Then are they glad because they be quiet; so he bringeth them unto their desired haven.
Isaiah 43:2	When thou passest through the waters, I will be with thee; and through the rivers, they shall not overflow thee: when thou walkest through the fire, thou shalt not be burned; neither shall the flame kindle upon thee.
Matthew 8:26	He said to them, "Why are you afraid, you men of little faith?" Then He got up and rebuked the winds and the sea, and it became perfectly calm.
Mark 4:39	And He got up and rebuked the wind and said to the sea, "Hush, be still." And the wind died down and it became perfectly calm.

Eyes and Ears

Psalms 91:3 — Surely he shall deliver thee from the snare of the fowler, and from the noisome (perilous or deadly) pestilence.

Psalms 146:8 — The LORD openeth the eyes of the blind: the LORD raiseth them that are bowed down: the LORD loveth the righteous.

Isaiah 29:18 — And in that day shall the deaf hear the words of the book, and the eyes of the blind shall see out of obscurity, and out of darkness.

Isaiah 35:5 — Then the eyes of the blind shall be opened, and the ears of the deaf shall be unstopped.

Isaiah 42:7 — To open the blind eyes, to bring out the prisoners from the prison, and them that sit in darkness out of the prison house.

Matthew 11:5 — The BLIND RECEIVE SIGHT and the lame walk, the lepers are cleansed and the deaf hear, the dead are raised up, and the POOR HAVE THE GOSPEL PREACHED TO THEM.

Hebrews 13:8 — Jesus Christ is same yesterday and today and forever.

Face

Psalms 30:2-3 — O LORD my God, I cried unto thee, and thou hast healed me. O LORD, thou hast brought up my soul from the grave: thou hast kept me alive, that I should not go down to the pit.

Psalms 34:5 — They looked unto him, and were lightened: and their faces were not ashamed.

Psalms 84:9 — Behold, O God our shield, and look on the face of your anointed.

Feet

I Samuel 2:4	The bows of the mighty men are broken, and they that stumbled are girded with strength.
I Samuel 2:9	He will keep the feet of his saints, and the wicked shall be silent in darkness; for by strength shall no man prevail.
Psalms 116:8-9	For thou hast delivered my soul from death, mine eyes from tears, and my feet from falling. I will walk before the LORD in the land of the living.
Psalms 121:3	He will not suffer thy foot to be moved: he that keepeth thee will not slumber.
Psalms 26:12	My foot standeth in an even place: in the congregations will I bless the LORD.

Fever

Matthew 8:17	This was to fulfill what was spoken through Isaiah the prophet: "HE HIMSELF TOOK OUR INFIRMITIES AND CARRIED AWAY OUR DISEASES."
Luke 4:39	And standing over her, He rebuked the fever, and it left her; and she immediately got up and waited on them.

Hands

Isaiah 35:3	Strengthen ye the weak hands, and confirm the feeble knees.
Hebrews 12:12-13	Therefore, strengthen the hands that are weak and the knees that are feeble, and make straight paths for your feet, so that the limb that is lame may not be put out of joint, but rather be healed.

Headaches

Psalms 25:18	Look upon mine affliction and my pain; and forgive all my sins.

Psalms 119:50	This is my comfort in my affliction: for thy word hath quickened me.
Psalms 119:107	I am afflicted very much: quicken me, O LORD, according unto thy word.

Heart Disease

Psalms 27:14	Wait on the LORD: be of good courage, and he shall strengthen thine heart: wait, I say, on the LORD.
Psalms 28:7	The LORD is my strength and my shield; my heart trusted in him, and I am helped: therefore my heart greatly rejoiceth; and with my song will I praise him.
Psalms 31:24	Be of good courage, and he shall strengthen your heart, all ye that hope in the LORD.
Psalms 73:26	My flesh and my heart faileth: But God is the strength of my heart, and my portion for ever.
Proverbs 4:23	Keep thy heart with all diligence; for out of it are the issues of life.
Proverbs 17:22	A merry heart doeth good like a medicine: but a broken spirit drieth the bones.

Hemorrhoids

Deuteronomy 28:27	The LORD will smite thee with the botch of Egypt, and with the emerods, and with the scab, and with the itch whereof thou canst be healed.
Galatians 3:13-14	Christ redeemed us from the curse of the Law, having become a curse for us – for it is written, "CURSED IS EVERYONE WHO HANGS ON A TREE" – in order that in Christ Jesus, the blessing of Abraham

might come to the Gentiles, so that we would receive the promise of the Spirit through faith.

Insomnia

Psalms 3:5	I laid me down and slept; I awakened; for the LORD sustained me.
Psalms 4:8	I will both lay down in peace, and sleep: for thou, LORD, only makest me dwell in safety.
Psalms 127:2	It is vain for you to rise up early, to sit up late, to eat the bread of sorrows: for so he giveth his beloved sleep.
Proverbs 3:24	When thou liest down, thou shalt not be afraid: yea, thou shalt lie down and thy sleep shall be sweet,
Ecclesiastes 5:12	The sleep of a labouring man is sweet, whether he eat little or much: but the abundance of the rich will not suffer him to sleep.
Isaiah 29:10	For the LORD hath poured out upon you the spirit of deep sleep, and hath closed your eyes: the prophets and your rulers, the seers hath he covered.

Kidneys

Psalms 69:15	Let not the waterflood overflow me, neither let the deep swallow me up, and let not the pit shut her mouth upon me.
Psalms 119:107	I am afflicted very much: quicken me, O LORD, according unto thy word.
Psalms 119:153	Consider mine affliction, and deliver me: for I do not forget thy law.
Psalms 144:7	Send thine hand from above; rid me, and deliver me out of great waters, from the hand of strange children.

Jeremiah 17:14	Heal me, O LORD, and I shall be healed; save me, and I shall be saved: for thou art my praise.
Isaiah 53:5	But he was wounded for our transgressions, he was bruised for our iniquities: the chastisement of our peace was upon him; and with his stripes we are healed.

Medication

Proverbs 4:20-22	My son, attend to my words; incline thine ear unto my sayings. Let them not depart from thine eyes; keep them in the midst of thine heart. For they are life unto those that find them, and health to all their flesh.
Isaiah 38:21	For Isaiah had said, "Let them take a lump of figs, and lay it for a plaister upon the boil, and he shall recover."
Luke 10:33-34	"But a Samaritan, who was on a journey, came upon him; and when he saw him, he felt compassion, and came to him and bandaged up his wounds, pouring oil and wine on them; and he put him on his own beast, and brought him to an inn and took care of him."

Mental

Psalms 9:9	The LORD also will be a refuge for the oppressed, a refuge in times of trouble.
Psalms 25:16-17	Turn thee unto me, and have mercy upon me; for I am desolate and afflicted. The troubles of my heart are enlarged: O bring thou me out of my distresses.
Psalms 25:20	O keep my soul, and deliver me: let me not be ashamed; for I put my trust in thee.
Psalms 37:23-24	The steps of a good man are ordered by the LORD: and he delighteth in his way. Though he fall, he shall not be utterly cast down: for the LORD upholdeth him with his hand.

Psalms 94:19	In the multitude of my thoughts within me thy comforts delight my soul.
Proverbs 16:3	Commit thy works unto the LORD, and thy thoughts shall be established.
Isaiah 50:7	For the Lord GOD will help me; therefore shall I not be confounded: therefore have I set my face like a flint, and I know that I shall not be ashamed.
I Corinthians 2:16	FOR WHO HAS KNOWN THE MIND OF THE LORD, THAT HE WILL INSTRUCT HIM? But we have the mind of Christ.
II Corinthians 10:5	We are destroying speculations and every lofty thing raised up against the knowledge of God, and we are taking every thought captive to the obedience of Christ.
Philippians 2:4-5	Do not merely look out for your own personal interests, but also for the interests of others. Have this attitude in yourselves which was also in Christ Jesus.
Philippians 4:7	And the peace of God which surpasses all comprehension will guard your hearts and your minds in Christ Jesus.
II Timothy 1:7	For God has not given us a spirit of timidity, but of power and love and discipline.

Mouth

Proverbs 10:11	The mouth of a righteous man is a well of life: but violence covereth the mouth of the wicked.
Proverbs 21:23	Whoso keepeth his mouth and his tongue keepeth his soul from troubles.
Luke 21:14-15	"So make up your minds not to prepare before hand to defend yourselves; for I will give you utterance and wisdom which none of your opponents will be able to resist or refute.

Romans 10:8-10	But what does it say? "THE WORD IS NEAR YOU, IN YOUR MOUTH AND IN YOUR HEART" – that is, the word of faith which we are preaching, that if you confess with your mouth Jesus as Lord, and believe in your heart that God raised Him from the dead, you will be saved; for with the heart a person believes, resulting in righteousness, and with the mouth he confesses, resulting in salvation.

Nervous Condition

Psalms 46:1	God is our refuge and strength, a very present help in trouble.
Psalms 55:22	Cast thy burden upon the LORD, and he shall sustain thee: he shall never suffer the righteous to be moved.
Psalms 116:1	I love the LORD, because he hath heard my voice and my supplications.
Psalms 119:17	Deal bountifully with thy servant, that I may live, and keep thy word.
Proverbs 3:26	For the LORD shall be thy confidence, and shall keep thy foot from being taken.
Romans 8:11	But if the Spirit of Him who raised Jesus from the dead dwells in you, He who raised Christ Jesus from the dead will also give life to your mortal bodies through His Spirit who dwells in you.
II Thessalonians 3:3	But the Lord is faithful, and He will strengthen and protect you from the evil one.

Pain

Psalms 25:18	Look upon my affliction and my pain; and forgive all my sins.

Jeremiah 17:14	Heal me, O LORD, and I shall be healed; save me, and I shall be saved: for thou art my praise.
James 5:14-15	Is anyone among you sick? Then he must call for the elders of the church and they are to pray over him, anointing him with oil in the name of the Lord; and the prayer offered in faith will restore the one who is sick, and the Lord will raise him up, and if he has committed sins, they will be forgiven him.

Poisoning

Mark 16:17-18	"These signs will accompany those who have believed: in My name they will cast out demons, they will speak with new tongues; they will pick up serpents, and if they drink any deadly poison, it will not hurt them; they will lay hands on the sick, and they will recover."
Luke 10:19	"Behold, I have given you authority to tread on serpents and scorpions, and over all the power of the enemy, and nothing will injure you."

Skin

Job 10:11	Thou hast clothed me with skin and flesh, and hast fenced me with bones and sinews.
Isaiah 43:2	When thou passest through the waters, I will be with thee; and through the rivers, they shall not overflow thee: when thou walkest through the fire, thou shalt not be burned; neither shall the flame kindle upon thee.

Sleepiness

Psalms 132:3-5	Surely I will not come into the tabernacle of my house, nor go up into my bed; I will not give sleep to mine eyes, or slumber to mine eyelids, until I find out a place for the LORD, an habitation for the mighty God of Jacob.

Proverbs 20:13	Love not sleep, lest thou come to poverty; open thine eyes, and thou shalt be satisfied with bread.
Romans 13:10-11	Love does no wrong to a neighbor; therefore love is the fulfillment of the law. Do this, knowing the time, that it is already the hour for you to awaken from sleep; for now salvation is nearer to us than when we believed.
I Thessalonians 5:2,6	For you yourselves know full well that the day of the Lord will come just like a thief in the night. So then let us not sleep as others do, but let us be alert and sober.

Strokes

I Samuel 2:4	The bows of the mighty men are broken, and they that stumbled are girded with strength.
Psalms 56:13	For thou hast delivered my soul from death: wilt not thou deliver my feet from falling, that I may walk before God in the light of the living?
Psalms 115:7	They have hands, but they handle not: feet have they, but they walk not: neither speak they through their throat.

(Claim the next scripture)

Psalms 116:8-9	For thou hast delivered my soul from death, mine eyes from tears, and my feet from falling. I will walk before the LORD in the land of the living.
Psalms 138:3	In the day when I cried thou answeredst me, and strengthenedst me with strength in my soul.
Psalms 139:14-15	I will praise thee; for I am fearfully and wonderfully made: marvelous are thy works; and that my soul knoweth right well. My substance was not hid from thee, when I was made in secret, and curiously wrought in the lowest parts of the earth.

Psalms 145:14	The LORD upholdeth all that fall, and raiseth up all those that be bowed down.
Proverbs 3:23	Then shalt thou walk in thy way safely, and thy foot shall not stumble.
Proverbs 4:12	When thou goest, thy steps shall not be straitened; and when thou runnest, thou shalt not stumble.

Stuttering

Isaiah 32:4	The heart also of the rash shall understand knowledge, and the tongue of the stammerers shall be ready to speak plainly.
Mark 7:35	And his ears were opened, and the impediment of his tongue was removed, and he began speaking plainly.

Teeth

Song of Solomon 4:2	Thy teeth are like a flock of sheep that are even shorn, which came up from the washing; whereof every one bear twins, and none is barren among them.

Tiredness / Weakness

Psalms 138:7	Though I walk in the midst of trouble, thou wilt revive me: thou shalt stretch forth thine hand against the wrath of mine enemies, and thy right hand shall save me.
Psalms 139:3	Thou compassest my path and my lying down, and art acquainted with all my ways.
Isaiah 40:29	He giveth power to the faint; and to them that have no might he increaseth strength.
Matthew 8:17	This was to fulfill what was spoken through Isaiah the prophet: "HE HIMSELF TOOK OUR INFIRMITIES AND CARRIED AWAY OUR DISEASES."

Romans 8:26　　In the same way the Spirit also helps our weakness; for we do not know how to pray as we should, but the Spirit Himself intercedes for us with groanings too deep for words.

Ulcers-Wounds

Psalms 147:3　　He healeth the broken in heart, and bindeth up their wounds.

Isaiah 30:26　　Moreover the light of the moon shall be as the light of the sun, and the light of the sun shall be sevenfold, as the light of seven days, in the day that the LORD bindeth up the breach of his people, and healeth the stroke of their wound.

Warts

Matthew 15:13　　But he answered and said, "Every plant which My heavenly Father did not plant, shall be uprooted."

Water Retention

Psalms 69:15　　Let not the waterflood overflow me, neither let the deep swallow me up, and let not the pit shut her mouth upon me.

Psalms 144:7-8　　Send thine hand from above; rid me, and deliver me out of great waters, from the hand of strange children; whose mouth speaketh vanity, and their right hand is a right hand of falsehood.

Heartache

Psalms 28:7　　The LORD is my strength and my shield; my heart trusted in him, and I am helped: therefore my heart greatly rejoiceth; and with my song will I praise him.

Psalms 34: 18	The LORD is nigh unto them that are of a broken heart; and saveth such as be of a contrite spirit.
Psalms 147:3	He healeth the broken in heart, and bindeth up their wounds.
Proverbs 4:23	Keep thy heart with all diligence; for out of it are the issues of life.
Proverbs 15:13	A merry heart maketh a cheerful countenance: but by sorrow of the heart the spirit is broken.

Intercession

Isaiah 58:12	And they that shall be of thee shall build the old waste places: thou shalt raise up the foundations of many generations; and thou shalt be called, The repairer of the breach, The restorer of paths to dwell in.
Isaiah 59:16	And he saw that there was no man, and wondered that there was no intercessor: therefore his arm brought salvation unto him; and his righteousness, it sustained him.
Isaiah 64: 7	And there is none that calleth upon thy name, that stirreth up himself to take hold of thee: for thou hast hid thy face from us, and hast consumed us, because of our iniquities.
Ezekiel 13:5	Ye have not gone up into the gaps, neither made up the hedge for the house of Israel to stand in the battle in the day of the LORD.
Romans 8:26-27	In the same way the Spirit also helps our weakness; for we do not know how to pray as we should, but the Spirit Himself intercedes for us with groanings too deep for words; and He who searches the hearts knows what the mind of the Spirit is, because He intercedes for the saints according to the will of God.

Galatians 6:2	Bear one another's burdens, and thereby fulfill the law of Christ.
I Timothy 2:1	First of all, then, I urge that entreaties and prayers, petitions, and thanksgivings, be made on behalf of all men.

Judgment

When I judge someone, I am in effect saying to God, "Move over, I'll judge this person according to my standards, and not God's."

John 7:24	"Do not judge according to appearance, but judge with righteous judgment."
Romans 14:13	Therefore let us not judge one another anymore, but rather determine this – not to put an obstacle or a stumbling block in a brother's way.
I Corinthians 4:3-5	But to me it is a very small thing that I may be examined by you, or by any human court; in fact I do not even examine myself. For I am conscious of nothing against myself, yet I am not by this acquitted; but the one who examines me is the Lord. Therefore do not go on passing judgment before the time, but wait until the Lord comes who will both bring to light the things hidden in the darkness and disclose the motives of men's hearts; and then each man's praise will come to him from God.
James 2:13	For judgment will be merciless to one who has shown no mercy; mercy triumphs over judgment.
Romans 12:10	Be devoted to one another in brotherly love; give preference to one another in honor.
I Corinthians 10:12	Therefore let him who thinks he stands take heed that he does not fall.
Ephesians 4:32	Be kind to one another, tender hearted, forgiving each other, just as God in Christ has forgiven you.

Romans 2:1 Therefore you have no excuse, everyone of you who passes judgment, for in that which you judge another, you condemn yourself; for you who judge practice the same things.

Judging-The gift of Prophecy

Proverbs 13:15 Good understanding giveth favor: but the way of transgressors is hard.

Matthew 7:16-20 " "You will know them by their fruits. Grapes are not gathered from thorn bushes nor figs from thistles, are they? So every good tree bears good fruit, but the bad tree bears bad fruit. A good tree cannot produce bad fruit, nor can a bad tree produce good fruit. Every tree that does not bear good fruit is cut down and thrown into the fire. So then, you will know them by their fruit."

Romans 8:15 For you have not received a spirit of slavery leading to fear again, but you have received a spirit of adoption as sons by which we cry out, "Abba! Father!"

I Corinthians 12:3 Therefore I make known to you that no one speaking by the Spirit of God says, "Jesus is accursed;" And no one can say, "Jesus is Lord," except by the Holy Spirit

I Corinthians 14:6 But now, brethren, if I come to you speaking in tongues, what will I profit you unless I speak to you either by way of revelation or of knowledge or of prophecy or of teaching?

I Thessalonians 5:19-22
Do not quench the Spirit; do not despise prophetic utterances. But examine everything carefully; hold fast to that which is good; abstain from every form of evil.

II Peter 1:20-21 But know this first of all, that no prophecy of Scripture is a matter of one's own interpretation, for no prophecy was ever made by an act of human will, but men moved by the Holy Spirit spoke from God.

Revelation 19:10 Then I fell at his feet to worship him. But he said to me, "Do not do that; I am a fellow servant of yours and your brethren who hold the testimony of Jesus; worship God. For the testimony of Jesus is the spirit of prophecy."

Judging-Prophets

Matthew 7:20-22 "So then, you will know them by their fruits. Not everyone who says to Me, Lord, Lord, will enter the kingdom of heaven, but he who does the will of My Father who is in heaven, will enter. Many will say to Me on that day,'Lord, Lord, did we not prophecy in Your name, and in Your name cast out demons, and in Your name perform many miracles?"

I Corinthians 14:32 And the spirits of prophets are subject to prophets.

I Thessalonians 5:19-21
Do not quench the Spirit; do not despise prophetic utterances. But examine everything carefully; hold fast to that which is good.

I John 4:1-3 Beloved, do not believe every spirit, but test the spirits to see whether they are from God, because many false prophets have gone out into the world. By this you know the Spirit of God: every spirit that confesses that Jesus Christ has come in the flesh is from God; and every spirit that does not confess Jesus is not from God; this is the spirit of the antichrist, of which you have heard that it is coming, and now it is already in the world.

Matthew 6:33 "But seek first His kingdom and His righteousness, and all these things will be added to you."

Colossians 1:12-13	Giving thanks to the Father, who has qualified us to share in the inheritance of the saints in Light. For He rescued us from the domain of darkness, and transferred us to the kingdom of His beloved Son.

Kingdom of God

Psalms 29:11	The LORD will give strength unto his people; the LORD will bless his people with peace.
Isaiah 26:2-3	Open ye the gates, that the righteous nation which keepeth the truth may enter in. Thou wilt keep him in perfect peace, whose mind is stayed on thee: because he trusteth in thee.
Isaiah 26:12	LORD, thou wilt ordain peace for us: for thou also hast wrought all our works in us.
Isaiah 32:17-18	And the work of righteousness shall be peace; and the effect of righteousness quietness and assurance for ever. And my people shall dwell in a peaceable habitation, and in sure dwellings, and in quiet resting places.
Jeremiah 15:16	Thy words were found, and I did eat them; and thy word was unto me the joy and rejoicing of mine heart: for I am called by thy name, O LORD God of hosts.
Matthew 6:33	"But seek first His kingdom and His righteousness, and all these things will be added to you."
Colossians 1:12-13	Giving thanks to the Father, who has qualified us to share in the inheritance of the saints in Light. For He rescued us from the domain of darkness, and transferred us to the kingdom of His beloved Son.

Keys to Kingdom of God

Matthew 16:19	"I will give you the keys of the kingdom of heaven; and whatever you bind on earth, shall have been bound in heaven, and whatever you loose on earth shall have been loosed in heaven."
Luke 10:19	"Behold, I have given you authority to tread on serpents and scorpions, and over all the power of the enemy, and nothing will injure you."
I John 3:8	The one who practices sin is of the devil; for the devil has sinned from the beginning. The Son of God appeared for this purpose, to destroy the works of the devil.

Laying on of Hands for Blessing

Genesis 48:14	And Israel stretched out his right hand, and laid it upon Ephraim's head, who was the younger, and his left hand upon Manasseh's head, guiding his hands wittingly; for Manasseh was the first born. (Blessing of the Family)
Exodus 17:11	And it came to pass, when Moses held up his hand, that Israel prevailed: and when he let down his hand, Amalek prevailed.
Deuteronomy 34:9	And Joshua, the son of Nun, was full of the spirit of wisdom; for Moses had laid his hands upon him: and the children of Israel hearkened unto him, and did as the Lord commanded Moses. (Prayer for Blessing)
Psalms 134:2	Lift up your hands in the sanctuary, and bless the LORD.
Psalms 141:2	Let my prayer be set forth before thee as incense; and the lifting up of my hands as the evening sacrifice. (Prayer of Worship)
Matthew 19:13-14	Then some children were brought to Him so that He

might lay His hands on them and pray; and the disciples rebuked them. But Jesus said, "Let the children alone, and do not hinder them from coming to Me; for the kingdom of heaven belongs to such as these."
(Jesus Blessed the Children)

Mark 16:17-18   "These signs will accompany those who have believed: in My name they will cast out demons, they will speak with new tongues; they will pick up serpents, and if they drink any deadly poison it will not hurt them; they will lay hands on the sick, and they will recover."
(Prayer for Healing)

Acts 6:3   "Therefore brethren, select from among you seven men of good reputation, full of the Spirit and of wisdom, whom we may put in charge of this task."

Acts 6:6   And these they brought before the apostles; and after praying, they laid their hands on them.
(Prayer for Ordination)

Acts 13:3   Then, when they had fasted and prayed and laid their hands on them, they sent them away.
(Prayer for Commissioning)

Acts 8:17   Then they began laying their hands on them, and they were receiving the Holy Spirit.
(Prayer for the Baptism of Holy Spirit)

Acts 19:11-12   God was performing extraordinary miracles, by the hands of Paul, so that handkerchiefs or aprons were even carried from his body to the sick, and the diseases left them and the evil spirits went out.
(Prayer for Miracles)

Galatians 2:9   And recognizing the grace that had been given to me, James and Cephas and John, who were reputed to be pillars, gave to me and Barnabas the right

	hand of fellowship, so that we might go to the Gentiles and they to the circumcised. (Prayer of Partnership and Fellowship)
I Timothy 2:8	Therefore I want the men in every place to pray, lifting up Holy hands without wrath and dissension. (Prayer for Discernment)
II Timothy 1:6	For this reason I remind you to kindle afresh the gift of God, which is in you through the laying on of my hands. (Prayer for Encouragement to Use Gifts of the Holy Spirits)
Hebrews 6:1-3	Therefore leaving the elementary teaching about the Christ, let us press on to maturity, not laying again a foundation of repentance from dead works and of faith toward God, of instruction about washings and laying on of hands, and the resurrection of the dead and eternal judgment. And this we will do, if God permits.

Learning

Deuteronomy 4:5	Behold, I have taught you statutes and judgments, even as the LORD my God commanded me, that ye should do so in the land whither ye go to possess it.
Psalms 119:66	Teach me good judgment and knowledge: for I have believed thy commandments.
Daniel 1:17	As for these four children, God gave them knowledge and skill in all learning and wisdom: and Daniel had understanding in all visions and dreams.
Matthew 7:7	"Ask, and it will be given to you; seek, and you will find; knock, and it will be opened to you."
Matthew 11:29	"Take My yoke upon you and learn from Me, for I am gentle and humble in heart, and YOU WILL FIND REST FOR YOUR SOULS."

Matthew 21:22	"And all things you ask in prayer, believing, you will receive."
John 6:45	It is written in the prophets, 'AND THEY SHALL ALL BE TAUGHT OF GOD.' Everyone who has heard and learned from the Father, comes to Me.
John 14:26	"But the Helper, the Holy Spirit, whom the Father will send in My name, He will teach you all things, and bring to your remembrance all that I said to you."
Colossians 1:9-11	For this reason also, since the day we heard of it, we have not ceased to pray for you and to ask that you may be filled with the knowledge of His will in all spiritual wisdom and understanding, so that you will walk in a manner worthy of the Lord, to please Him in all respect, bearing fruit in every good work and increasing in the knowledge of God; strengthened with all power, according to His glorious might, for the attaining of all steadfastness and patience; joyously.

Lost Articles & People

Matthew 10:26	"Therefore do not fear them, for there is nothing concealed that will not be revealed, or hidden that will not be known."
Luke 8:17	"For nothing is hidden that will not become evident, nor anything secret that will not be known and come to light."

Love of Brethren

John 15:12	"This is My commandment that you love one another, just as I have loved you."
Romans 12:9-10	Let love be without hypocrisy. Abhor what is evil; cling to what is good. Be devoted to one another in brotherly love; give preference to one another in honor.

Romans 13:10	Love does no wrong to a neighbor; therefore love is the fulfillment of the law.
Romans 15:7	Therefore, accept one another, just as Christ also accepted us to the glory of God.
Galatians 5:13-15	For you were called to freedom, brethren; only do not turn your freedom into an opportunity for the flesh, but through love, serve one another. For the whole Law is fulfilled in one word, in the statement, "YOU SHALL LOVE YOUR NEIGHBOR AS YOURSELF." But if you bite and devour one another, take care that you are not consumed by one another.
Ephesians 4:32	Be kind to one another, tender-hearted, forgiving each other, just as God in Christ also has forgiven you.
Colossians 3:12-14	So, as those who have been chosen of God, Holy and beloved, put on a heart of compassion, kindness, humility, gentleness and patience; bearing with one another, and forgiving each other, whoever has a complaint against anyone; just as the Lord forgave you, so also should you. Beyond all these things, put on love, which is the perfect bond of unity.
I Thessalonians 3:12-13	And may the Lord cause you to increase and abound in love for one another, and for all people just as we also do for you; so that He may establish your hearts without blame in holiness before our God and Father at the coming of our Lord Jesus with all His saints.
I Thessalonians 5: 12-13	But what we request of you, brethren, that you appreciate those who diligently labor among you, and have charge over you in the Lord and give you instruction, and that you esteem them very highly in love because of their work. Live in peace with one another.

I Peter 1:22-23	Since you have in obedience to the truth, purified your souls for a sincere love of the brethren, fervently love one another from the heart, for you have been born again not of seed which is perishable but imperishable, that is, through the living and enduring word of God.
I John 4:7-8	Beloved, let us love one another, for love is from God; and everyone who loves is born of God and knows God. The one who does not love does not know God, for God is love.
I John 4:12	No one has seen God at any time; if we love one another, God abides in us, and His love is perfected in us.
I John 4:19-21	We love, because He first loved us. If someone says, "I love God," and hates his brother, he is a liar; for the one who does not love his brother whom he has seen, can not love God whom he has not seen. And this commandment we have from Him, that the one who loves God should love his brother also.

Love and Care of the Father

Psalms 145:20	The LORD preserveth all them that love him: but all the wicked will he destroy.
Proverbs 3:11-12	My son, despise not the chastening of the LORD; neither be weary of his correction: For whom the LORD loveth he correcteth; even as a father the son in whom he delighteth.
Isaiah 38:16-17	O Lord, by these things men live, and in all these things is the life of my spirit: so wilt thou recover me, and make me to live. Behold, for peace I had great bitterness: but thou hast in love to my soul delivered it from the pit of corruption: for thou hast cast all my sins behind thy back.

Jeremiah 31:3	The LORD hath appeared of old unto me, saying, Yea, I have loved thee with an everlasting love: therefore with lovingkindness have I drawn thee.
John 3:16-17	"For God so loved the world, that He gave His only begotten Son, that whoever believes in Him shall not perish, but have eternal life. For God did not send the Son into the world to judge the world, but that the world might be saved through Him."
John 14:21	"He who has my commandments and keeps them is the one who loves Me; and he who loves Me will be loved by My Father, and I will love Him and will disclose Myself to him."
Romans 5:5	And hope does not disappoint, because the love of God has been poured out within our hearts through the Holy Spirit who was given to us.
Romans 8:37	But in all these things we overwhelmingly conquer through Him who loved us.
Ephesians 2:4-6	But God, being rich in mercy, because of His great love with which He loved us, even when we were dead in our transgressions, made us alive together with Christ (by grace you have been saved), and raised us up with Him, and seated us with Him in the heavenly places in Christ Jesus.
Philippians 1:6	For I am confident of this very thing, that He who began a good work in you will perfect it until the day of Christ Jesus.
I Peter 5:7	Casting all your anxiety on Him, because He cares for you.
I John 4:9-11	By this the love of God was manifested in us, that God has sent His only begotten Son into the world so that we might live through Him. In this is love, not

	that we loved God, but that He loved us, and sent His son to be the propitiation for our sins. Beloved, if God so loved us, we also ought to love one another.
I John 4:16-19	We have come to know and have believed the love which God has for us. God is love, and the one who abides in love abides in God, and God abides in him. By this, love is perfected with us, so that we may have confidence in the day of judgment; because as He is, so also are we in this world. There is no fear in love; but perfect love casts out fear, because fear involves punishment, and the one who fears is not perfected in love. We love, because He first loved us.

Maintaining Deliverance

Psalms 23:4	Yea, though I walk through the valley of the shadow of death, I will fear no evil: for thou art with me; thy rod and thy staff they comfort me.
Psalms 34:9-10	O fear the LORD, ye his saints: for there is no want to them that fear him. The young lions do lack, and suffer hunger: but they that seek the LORD shall not want any good thing .
Psalms 46:1	God is our refuge and strength, a very present help in trouble.
Psalms 71:1	In thee, O LORD, do I put my trust: let me never be put to confusion.
Proverbs 3:26	For the LORD shall be thy confidence, and shall keep thy foot from being taken.
Isaiah 26:4	Trust ye in the LORD for ever: for in the LORD JEHOVAH is everlasting strength:
Isaiah 50:7	For the Lord GOD will help me; therefore shall I not be confounded: therefore have I set my face like a flint, and I know that I shall not be ashamed.

John 8:36	"So if the Son makes you free, you will be free indeed."
John 10:10	"The thief comes only to steal and kill and destroy; I came that they may have life, and have it abundantly."
Romans 8:32	He who did not spare His own Son, but delivered over for us all, how will He not also with Him, freely give us all things?
I Corinthians 6:17	But the one who joins himself to the Lord is one spirit with Him.
II Corinthians 3:17	Now the Lord is the Spirit, and where the Spirit of the Lord is, there is liberty.
Philippians 4:7	And the peace of God, which surpasses all comprehension, will guard your hearts and your minds in Christ Jesus.
Philippians 4:19	And my God will supply all your needs according to His riches in glory in Christ Jesus.
II Timothy 1:7	For God has not given us a spirit of timidity, but of power and love and discipline.

Marriages

Genesis 1:27	So God created man in his own image, in the image of God created he him; male and female created he them.
Genesis 2:18	And the LORD God said, "It is not good that the man should be alone; I will make him an help mate for him."
Genesis 2:24	Therefore shall a man leave his father and his mother, and shall cleave unto his wife: and they shall be one flesh.

Proverbs 5:18-19	Let thy fountain be blessed: and rejoice with the wife of thy youth. Let her be as the loving deer and pleasant doe; let her breasts satisfy thee at all times; and be thou ravished always with her love.
Proverbs 12:4	A virtuous woman is a crown to her husband: but she that maketh ashamed is as rottenness in his bones.
Proverbs 18:22	Whoso findeth a wife findeth a good thing, and obtaineth favor of the LORD.
Ecclesiastes 9:9	Live joyfully with the wife whom thou lovest all the days of the life of thy vanity, which he hath given thee under the sun, all the days of thy vanity: for that is thy portion in this life, and in thy labor which thou takest under the sun.
Matthew 19:3-6	Some Pharisees came to Jesus, testing Him and asking, "Is it lawful for a man to divorce his wife for any reason at all?" And He answered and said, "Have you not read that He who created them from the beginning MADE THEM MALE AND FEMALE, and said, 'FOR THIS REASON, A MAN SHALL LEAVE HIS FATHER AND MOTHER AND BE JOINED TO HIS WIFE, AND THE TWO SHALL BECOME ONE FLESH'? "So they are no longer two, but one flesh. What therefore God has joined together, let no man separate."
I Corinthians 7:2	But because of immoralities, each man is to have his own wife, and each woman is to have her own husband.
Ephesians 5:21-33	Be subject to one another in the fear of Christ. Wives, be subject to your own husbands, as to the Lord. For the husband is the head of the wife, as Christ also is the head of the church, He Himself being the Savior of the body. But as the church is subject to Christ, so also the wives ought to be to their

husbands in everything. Husbands, love your wives, just as also Christ loved the church and gave Himself up for her, so that He might sanctify her, having cleansed her by the washing of water with the word, that He might present to Himself the church in all her glory, having no spot or wrinkle or any such thing; but that she would be holy and blameless. So husbands ought also to love their own wives as their own bodies. He who loves his own wife loves himself; for no one ever hated his own flesh, but nourishes and cherishes it, just as Christ also does the church, because we are members of His body. FOR THIS REASON A MAN SHALL LEAVE HIS FATHER AND MOTHER AND SHALL BE JOINED TO HIS WIFE, AND THE TWO SHALL BECOME ONE FLESH. This mystery is great; but I am speaking with reference to Christ and the church. Nevertheless, each individual among you also is to love his own wife even as himself, and the wife must see to it that she respects her husband.

I Corinthians 13:4-8   Love is patient, love is kind and not jealous; love does not brag and is not arrogant, does not act unbecomingly; it does not seek its own, is not provoked, does not take into account a wrong suffered, does not rejoice in unrighteousness, but rejoices with the truth; bears all things, believes all things, hopes all things, endures all things. Love never fails; but if there are gifts of prophecy, they will be done away; if there are tongues, they will cease; if there is knowledge, it will be done away.

Philippians 2:2-4   Make my joy complete by being of the same mind, maintaining the same love, united in spirit, intent on one purpose. Do nothing from selfishness or empty conceit, but with humility of mind, regard one another as more important than yourselves; do not merely look out for your own personal interests, but also for the interests of others.

Hebrews 13:4	Marriage is to be held in honor among all, and the marriage bed is to be undefiled; for fornicators and adulterers, God will judge.
Colossians 3:18-19	Wives, be subject to your husbands, as is fitting in the Lord. Husbands, love your wives and do not be embittered against them.

Marriage is a beautiful partnership given by God, between man and woman. It is meant to join a couple as companions. God did not take woman from man's feet or head to have him lord it over her or be trampled underneath him. God took woman from man's rib to be beside him. She is to love him and help him and he is to love her and help her. God did not create woman separately from man. God created woman from man, and this reveals to us God's plan that he meant for the two of them to be together.

Oppression

Job 36:15	He delivereth the poor in his affliction, and openeth their ears in oppression.
Psalms 9:9-10	The LORD also will be a refuge for the oppressed, a refuge in times of trouble. And they that know thy name will put their trust in thee: for thou, LORD, hast not forsaken them that seek thee.
Psalms 119:121	I have done judgment and justice: leave me not to mine oppressors.
Acts 10:38	"You know of Jesus of Nazareth, how God anointed Him with the Holy Spirit and with power, and how He went about doing good and healing all who were oppressed by the devil, for God was with Him."

Overcoming the Powers of Darkness

Ephesians 1:7	In Him we have redemption through His blood, the

	forgiveness of our trespasses, according to the riches of His grace.
I John 1:7	But if we walk in the Light as He Himself is in the Light, we have fellowship with one another, and the blood of Jesus His Son cleanses us from all sin.
Romans 5:9	Much more then, having now been justified by His blood, we shall be saved from the wrath of God through Him.
II Corinthians 5:21	He made Him who knew no sin to be sin on our behalf, so that we might become the righteousness of God in Him.
Hebrews 13:12	Therefore Jesus also, that He might sanctify the people through His own blood, suffered outside the gate.
I Corinthians 3:16	Do you not know that you are a temple of God and that the Spirit of God dwells in you?
II Corinthians 7:1	Therefore, having these promises, beloved, let us cleanse ourselves from all defilement of the flesh and spirit, perfecting holiness in the fear of God.

Patience

Ecclesiastes 7:8	Better is the end of a thing than the beginning thereof: and the patient in spirit is better than the proud in spirit.
Proverbs 16:32	He that is slow to anger is better than the mighty; and he that ruleth his spirit than he that taketh a city.
Isaiah 30:15	For thus saith the Lord GOD, the Holy One of Israel; In returning and rest shall ye be saved; in quietness and in confidence shall be your strength and ye would not.

Luke 8:15	But the seed in the good soil, these are the ones who have heard the word in an honest and good heart, and hold it fast, and bear fruit with perseverance.
Luke 21:19	By your endurance you will gain your lives.
Romans 5:3-5	And not only this, but we also exult in our tribulations, knowing that tribulation brings about perseverance; and perseverance, proven character; and proven character, hope; and hope does not disappoint, because the love of God has been poured out within our hearts through the Holy Spirit who was given to us.
Hebrews 10:36	For you have need of endurance, so that when you have done the will of God, you may receive what was promised.
Hebrews 12:1	Therefore, since we have so great a cloud of witnesses surrounding us, let us also lay aside every encumbrance and the sin which so easily entangles us, and let us run with endurance the race that is set before us,
James 1:2-3	Consider it all joy, my brethren, when you encounter various trials, knowing that the testing of your faith produces endurance.
James 5:7-8	Therefore be patient, brethren, until the coming of the Lord. The farmer waits for the precious produce of the soil, being patient about it, until it gets the early and late rains. You too be patient; strengthen your hearts, for the coming of the Lord is near.
I Peter 2:20	For what credit is there if, when you sin and are harshly treated, you endure it with patience? But if when you do what is right and suffer for it you patiently endure it, this finds favor with God.
Revelation 3:10	Because you have kept the word of My perseverance, I also will keep you from the hour of testing, that

hour which is about to come upon the whole world, to test those who dwell on the earth.

Peace

Psalms 29:11   The LORD will give strength unto his people; the LORD will bless his people with peace.

Psalm 55:18   He hath delivered my soul in peace from the battle that was against me: for there were many with [confronting against] me.

Proverbs 3:1-2   My son, forget not my law; but let thine heart keep my commandments: For length of days, and long life, and peace, shall they add to thee.

Isaiah 26:3   Thou wilt keep him in perfect peace, whose mind is stayed on thee: because he trusteth in thee.

Isaiah 26:12   LORD, thou wilt ordain peace for us: for thou also hast wrought all our works in us.

Isaiah 32:17   And the work of righteousness shall be peace; and the effect of righteousness, quietness, and assurance for ever.

Philippians 4:7   And the peace of God, which surpasses all comprehension, will guard your hearts and your minds in Christ Jesus.

II Thessalonians 3:16   Now may the Lord of peace Himself continually grant you peace in every circumstance. The Lord be with you all!

Pharmakeia- Sorcery, Enchantment by Drugs or Magic, All are Abominations that God Hates

Leviticus 19:26   Ye shall not eat any thing with the blood: neither shall ye use enchantment, nor observe times.

Leviticus 19:28   Ye shall not make any cuttings in your flesh for the dead, nor print any marks (Tattoo) upon you: I am the LORD.

Leviticus 19:31   Regard not them that have familiar spirits, neither seek after wizards, to be defiled by them: I am the LORD your God.

Deuteronomy 7:25-26   The graven images of their gods shall ye burn with fire: thou shalt not desire the silver or gold that is on them, nor take it unto thee, lest thou be snared therein: for it is an abomination to the LORD thy God. Neither shalt thou bring an abomination into thine house, lest thou be a cursed thing like it: but thou shalt utterly detest it, and thou shalt utterly abhor it; for it is a cursed thing.

Deuteronomy 18:10-12
There shall not be found among you any one that maketh his son or his daughter to pass through the fire, or that useth divination, or an observer of times, or an enchanter, or a witch, or a charmer, or a consulter with familiar spirits, or a wizard, or a necromancer. For all that do these things are an abomination unto the LORD: and because of these abominations the LORD thy God doth drive them out from before thee.

Micah 5:11-14   And I will cut off the cities of thy land, and throw down all thy strong holds: And I will cut off witchcrafts out of thine hand; and thou shalt have no more soothsayers: Thy graven images also will I cut off, and thy standing images out of the midst of thee; and thou shalt no more worship the work of thine hands. And I will pluck up thy groves out of the midst of thee: so will I destroy thy cities. And I will execute vengeance in anger and fury upon the heathen, such as they have not heard.

Colossians 1:17-18	He is before all things, and in Him all things hold together. He is also head of the body, the church. He is the beginning, the firstborn from the dead, so that He Himself will come to have first place in everything.
Revelation 21:8	"But for the cowardly and unbelieving and abominable and murderers and immoral persons and sorcerers and idolaters and all liars, their part will be in the lake that burns with fire and brimstone, which is the second death."

Poverty

Job 36:11-12	If they obey and serve him, they shall spend their days in prosperity, and their years in pleasures. But if they obey not, they shall perish by the sword, and they shall die without knowledge.
Job 36:15	He delivereth the poor in his affliction, and openeth their ears in oppression.
Psalms 2:8	Ask of me, and I shall give thee the heathen for thine inheritance, and the uttermost parts of the earth for thy possession.
Psalms 34:9-10	O fear the LORD, ye his saints: for there is no want to them that fear him. The young lions do lack, and suffer hunger: but they that seek the LORD shall not want any good thing.
Psalms 37:4	Delight thyself also in the LORD; and he shall give thee the desires of thine heart.
Psalms 55:22	Cast thy burden upon the LORD, and he shall sustain thee: he shall never suffer the righteous to be moved.
Psalms 68:19	Blessed be the Lord, who daily loadeth us with benefits, even the God of our salvation. Selah.
Proverbs 8:21	That I may cause those that love me to inherit substance; and I will fill their treasures.

Proverbs 10:4	He becometh poor that dealeth with a slack hand: but the hand of the diligent maketh rich.
Matthew 6:33	But seek first His kingdom and His righteousness, and all these things will be added to you.
John 14:13	Whatever you ask in My name, that will I do, so that the Father may be glorified in the Son.
II Corinthians 8:9	For you know the grace of our Lord Jesus Christ, that though He was rich, yet for your sake He became poor, so that you through His poverty might become rich.
Philippians 4:6	Be anxious for nothing, but in everything by prayer and supplication with thanksgiving let your requests be made known to God.
Philippians 4:19	And my God will supply all your needs according to His riches in glory in Christ Jesus.

Praise and Thanks

Psalms 33:1	Rejoice in the LORD, O ye righteous: for praise is comely for the upright.
Psalms 50:23	Whoso offereth praise glorifieth me: and to him that ordereth his conversation aright will I shew the salvation of God.
Psalms 135:1	Praise ye the LORD. Praise ye the name of the LORD; praise him, O ye servants of the LORD.
Psalms 135:3	Praise the LORD; for the LORD is good: sing praises unto his name; for it is pleasant.
Psalms 136:1	O give thanks unto the LORD; for he is good: for his mercy endureth for ever.

Psalms 138:1	I will praise thee with my whole heart: before the gods will I sing praise unto thee.
Psalms 145:1	I will extol thee, my God, O king; and I will bless thy name for ever and ever.
Psalms 145:2	Every day will I bless thee; and I will praise thy name for ever and ever.
Psalms 146:1-2	Praise ye the LORD. Praise the LORD, O my soul. While I live will I praise the LORD: I will sing praises unto my God while I have any being.

Use all of Psalms 148 and 149 and 150 to praise God. He delights in our praise and thanksgiving and will bless us abundantly the more we praise Him for what He has done for us.

Isaiah 25:1	O LORD, thou art my God; I will exalt thee, I will praise thy name; for thou hast done wonderful things; thy counsels of old are faithfulness and truth.
Philippians 4:6	Be anxious for nothing, but in everything by prayer and supplication with thanksgiving let your requests be made known to God.
I Thessalonians 5:18	In everything give thanks; for this is God's will for you in Christ Jesus.
Hebrews 13:15	Through Him then, let us continually offer up a sacrifice of praise to God, that is, the fruit of lips that give thanks to His name.
I Peter 2:9	But you are A CHOSEN RACE, A royal PRIESTHOOD, A HOLY NATION, A PEOPLE FOR God's OWN POSSESSION, so that you may proclaim the excellencies of Him who has called you out of darkness into His marvelous light;

Prayer

Prayer is a conversation with God. It is a song of praise, a petition, a supplication, a cry for God to hear us. It can be just a word spoken, a thought raised, or a shout given.

God hears them all. God fervently desires to hear from us and wants us to listen to Him in prayer.

Even the silent prayers in our hearts are clearly heard by God.

Some of our best prayer is done while doing our common ordinary things, like taking care of the family, or driving to work. When we see things in our every day life and give God praise, and thanksgiving for helping us with all the many tasks that we have to do, He rejoices with us, and our jobs seems easier.

We praise Him with our smiles and laughter and touch Him with our tears and sadness as He is as close as whispering His name. As believers, His Spirit dwells in us and He will never leave us.

In our weakness, as we call out to Him, He draws us closer and strengthens us with the help and nearness of those around us who pray for us.

I Kings 8:28	Yet have thou respect unto the prayer of thy servant, and to his supplication, O LORD my God, to hearken unto the cry and to the prayer, which thy servant prayeth before thee today.
Psalms 4:3	But know that the LORD hath set apart him that is godly for himself: the LORD will hear when I call unto him.
Psalms 5:2	Hearken unto the voice of my cry, my King, and my God: for unto thee will I pray.
Psalms 54:2	Hear my prayer, O God; give ear to the words of my mouth.
Psalms 55:1	Give ear to my prayer, O God; and hide not thyself from my supplication.
Isaiah 55:6	Seek ye the LORD while he may be found, call ye upon him while he is near:

Isaiah 65:24	And it shall come to pass, that before they call, I will answer; and while they are yet speaking, I will hear.
Acts 12:5	So Peter was kept in the prison, but prayer for him was being made fervently by the church to God.
Romans 12:12	... rejoicing in hope, persevering in tribulation, devoted to prayer,
II Corinthians 1:10-11	... who delivered us from so great a peril of death, and will deliver us, He on whom we have set our hope. And He will yet deliver us, you also joining in helping us through your prayers, so that thanks may be given by many persons on our behalf for the favor bestowed on us through the prayers of many.
Ephesians 6:18	With all prayer and petition pray at all times in the Spirit, and with this in view, be on the alert with all perseverance and petition for all the saints,
Philippians 4:6	Be anxious for nothing, but in everything by prayer and supplication with thanksgiving let your requests be made known to God.
James 5:13-15	Is anyone among you suffering? Then he must pray. Is anyone cheerful? He is to sing praises. Is anyone among you sick? Then he must call for the elders of the church and they are to pray over him, anointing him with oil in the name of the Lord; and the prayer offered in faith will restore the one who is sick, and the Lord will raise him up, and if he has committed sins, they will be forgiven him.
Jude 20	But you, beloved, building yourselves up on your most holy faith, praying in the Holy Spirit,

Pride

Pride is our boastful attitude in telling God that we don't need him.

Psalms 138:6	Though the LORD be high, yet hath he respect unto the lowly: but the proud he knoweth afar off.
Proverbs 11:2	When pride cometh, then cometh shame: but with the lowly is wisdom.
Proverbs 16:18	Pride goeth before destruction, and an haughty spirit before a fall.
Mark 7:21-23	"For from within, out of the heart of men, proceed the evil thoughts, fornications, thefts, murders, adulteries, deeds of coveting and wickedness, as well as deceit, sensuality, envy, slander, pride and foolishness. All these evil things proceed from within and defile the man."
I John 2:16	For all that is in the world, the lust of the flesh and the lust of the eyes and the boastful pride of life, is not from the Father, but is from the world.

Prosperity

God wants us to be debt free so that our hearts are free to love. When we are worried about our own needs and finances, we aren't so concerned with the needs of the least of our brothers and sisters. When your dreams and goals do not match the size of your paycheck then your dreams and goals are not from God, and you need to take them to him in prayer. He will help you to see what it is that He wants for you, and there usually is a difference.

Job 36:11	If they obey and serve him, they shall spend their days in prosperity, and their years in pleasures.
Psalms 34:9	O fear the LORD, ye his saints: for there is no want to them that fear him.
Proverbs 3:9-10	Honour the LORD with thy substance, and with the firstfruits of all thine increase: So shall thy barns

	be filled with plenty, and thy presses shall burst out with new wine.
Proverbs 28:13	He that covereth his sins shall not prosper: but whoso confesseth and forsaketh them shall have mercy.
Proverbs 28:27	He that giveth unto the poor shall not lack: but he that hideth his eyes shall have many a curse.
Jeremiah 29:11	For I know the thoughts that I think toward you, saith the LORD, thoughts of peace, and not of evil, to give you an expected end.
Malachi 3:10	Bring ye all the tithes into the storehouse, that there may be meat in mine house, and prove me now herewith, saith the LORD of hosts, if I will not open you the windows of heaven, and pour you out a blessing, that there shall not be room enough to receive it.
Philippians 4:19	And my God will supply all your needs according to His riches in glory in Christ Jesus.
III John 2	Beloved, I pray that in all respects you may prosper and be in good health, just as your soul prospers.

Protection

Psalms 5:11-12	But let all those that put their trust in thee rejoice: let them ever shout for joy, because thou defendest them: let them also that love thy name be joyful in thee. For thou, LORD, wilt bless the righteous; with favour wilt thou compass him as with a shield.
Psalms 32:7	Thou art my hiding place; thou shalt preserve me from trouble; thou shalt compass me about with songs of deliverance. Selah.
Psalms 34:20	He keepeth all his bones: not one of them is broken.

Psalms 41:1-2	Blessed is he that considereth the poor: the LORD will deliver him in time of trouble. The LORD will preserve him, and keep him alive; and he shall be blessed upon the earth: and thou wilt not deliver him unto the will of his enemies.
Psalms 46:1	God is our refuge and strength, a very present help in trouble.
Psalms 64:1	Hear my voice, O God, in my prayer: preserve my life from fear of the enemy.
Psalms 69:29	But I am poor and sorrowful: let thy salvation, O God, set me up on high.
Psalms 91:11	For he shall give his angels charge over thee, to keep thee in all thy ways.
Psalms 91:14-15	Because he hath set his love upon me, therefore will I deliver him: I will set him on high, because he hath known my name. He shall call upon me, and I will answer him: I will be with him in trouble; I will deliver him, and honour him.
Psalms 97:10	Ye that love the LORD, hate evil: he preserveth the souls of his saints; he delivereth them out of the hand of the wicked.
Psalms 116:6	The LORD preserveth the simple: I was brought low, and he helped me.
Psalms 121:8	The LORD shall preserve thy going out and thy coming in from this time forth, and even for evermore.
Psalms 145:18	The LORD is nigh unto all them that call upon him, to all that call upon him in truth.
Proverbs 1:33	But whoso hearkeneth unto me shall dwell safely, and shall be quiet from fear of evil.

Proverbs 3:25	Be not afraid of sudden fear, neither of the desolation of the wicked, when it cometh.
Isaiah 32:18	And my people shall dwell in a peaceable habitation, and in sure dwellings, and in quiet resting places.
John 17:15	I do not ask You to take them out of the world, but to keep them from the evil one.
Romans 8:37	But in all these things we overwhelmingly conquer through Him who loved us.
II Thessalonians 3:3	But the Lord is faithful, and He will strengthen and protect you from the evil one.

Rebellion

Against God's Word

Joshua 22:19	Notwithstanding, if the land of your possession be unclean, then pass ye over unto the land of the possession of the LORD, wherein the LORD'S tabernacle dwelleth, and take possession among us: but rebel not against the LORD, nor rebel against us, in building you an altar beside the altar of the LORD our God.
I Samuel 15:23	For rebellion is as the sin of witchcraft, and stubbornness is as iniquity and idolatry. Because thou hast rejected the word of the LORD, he hath also rejected thee from being king.
Psalms 107:10-12	Such as sit in darkness and in the shadow of death, being bound in affliction and iron; Because they rebelled against the words of God, and contemned (despised) the counsel of the most High: Therefore he brought down their heart with labour; they fell down, and there was none to help.
Proverbs 17:11	An evil man seeketh only rebellion: therefore a cruel messenger shall be sent against him.

Isaiah 1:20	But if ye refuse and rebel, ye shall be devoured with the sword: for the mouth of the LORD hath spoken it.

Against the Holy Spirit

Luke 1:17	"It is he who will go as a forerunner before Him in the spirit and power of Elijah, TO TURN THE HEARTS OF THE FATHERS BACK TO THE CHILDREN, and the disobedient to the attitude of the righteous, so as to make ready a people prepared for the Lord."
Ephesians 2:1-2	And you were dead in your trespasses and sins, in which you formerly walked according to the course of this world, according to the prince of the power of the air, of the spirit that is now working in the sons of disobedience.
Ephesians 5:6	Let no one deceive you with empty words, for because of these things the wrath of God comes upon the sons of disobedience.
Ephesians 5: 11-12	Do not participate in the unfruitful deeds of darkness, but instead even expose them; for it is disgraceful even to speak of the things which are done by them in secret.

Against God

Hebrews 3:12	Take care, brethren, that there not be in any one of you an evil, unbelieving heart that falls away from the living God.

God redeemed us through his Son: Titus 3:3-7 gives us an example.

For we also once were foolish ourselves, disobedient, deceived, enslaved to various lusts and pleasures, spending our life in malice and envy, hateful, hating one another. But when the kindness of God our Savior and His love for mankind appeared, He saved us, not on the basis of deeds which we have done in righteousness, but according to His mercy, by the washing of regeneration and renewing by the Holy Spirit, whom He poured out upon us richly through Jesus Christ our Savior, so that being justified by His grace we would be made heirs according to the hope of eternal life.

Righteousness

Psalms 23:3	He restoreth my soul: he leadeth me in the paths of righteousness for his name's sake.
Psalms 37: 25	I have been young, and now am old; yet have I not seen the righteous forsaken, nor his seed begging bread.
Psalms 84:11-12	For the LORD God is a sun and shield: the LORD will give grace and glory: no good thing will he withhold from them that walk uprightly. O LORD of hosts, blessed is the man that trusteth in thee.
Proverbs 10:11	The mouth of a righteous man is a well of life: but violence covereth the mouth of the wicked.
Proverbs 10:24	The fear of the wicked, it shall come upon him: but the desire of the righteous shall be granted.
Matthew 6:33	But seek first His kingdom and His righteousness, and all these things will be added to you.
Romans 3:21-22	But now apart from the Law the righteousness of God has been manifested, being witnessed by the Law and the Prophets, even the righteousness of God through faith in Jesus Christ for all those who believe; for there is no distinction.
Romans 5:19	For as through the one man's disobedience the many were made sinners, even so through the obedience of the One the many will be made righteous.
Romans 10:10	... for with the heart a person believes, resulting in righteousness, and with the mouth he confesses, resulting in salvation.

Romans 14:17	... for the kingdom of God is not eating and drinking, but righteousness and peace and joy in the Holy Spirit.
I Corinthians 1:30	But by His doing you are in Christ Jesus, who became to us wisdom from God, and righteousness and sanctification, and redemption.
Galatians 3:6	Even so Abraham BELIEVED GOD, AND IT WAS RECKONED TO HIM AS RIGHTEOUSNESS.
Philippians 3:9	And may be found in Him, not having a righteousness of my own derived from the Law, but that which is through faith in Christ, the righteousness which comes from God on the basis of faith.

Salvation

Salvation provides according to the Hebrew, Greek and Chaldee concordance:

Aid	Be made whole	Be safe
Defense	Deliverance	Do well
Freedom	Health	Healing
Help	Liberty	Preserve
Prosperity	Rescue	Safety
Victory		

There are seven major benefits that Salvation provides

1. Deliverance

Psalms 34:4	I sought the LORD, and he heard me, and delivered me from all my fears.
Psalms 34:7	The angel of the LORD encampeth round about them that fear him, and delivereth them.
Psalms 34:17	The righteous cry, and the LORD heareth, and delivereth them out of all their troubles.
Psalms 34:19	Many are the afflictions of the righteous: but the LORD delivereth him out of them all.

Psalms 50:15	And call upon me in the day of trouble: I will deliver thee, and thou shalt glorify me.
Psalms 91:3	Surely he shall deliver thee from the snare of the fowler, and from the noisome pestilence.
Psalms 91:14	Because he hath set his love upon me, therefore will I deliver him: I will set him on high, because he hath known my name.
Psalms 91:15	He shall call upon me, and I will answer him: I will be with him in trouble; I will deliver him, and honour him.
Proverbs 11:21	Though hand join in hand, the wicked shall not be unpunished: but the seed of the righteous shall be delivered.

2. Guidance

Psalms 25:9	The meek will he guide in judgment: and the meek will he teach his way.
Psalms 32:8	I will instruct thee and teach thee in the way which thou shalt go: I will guide thee with mine eye.
Proverbs 3:6	In all thy ways acknowledge him, and he shall direct thy paths.
Isaiah 58:11	And the LORD shall guide thee continually, and satisfy thy soul in drought, and make fat thy bones: and thou shalt be like a watered garden, and like a spring of water, whose waters fail not.
John 16:13	"But when He, the Spirit of truth, comes, He will guide you into all the truth; for He will not speak on His own initiative, but whatever He hears, He will speak; and He will disclose to you what is to come.

3. Healing

Exodus 23:25 — And ye shall serve the LORD your God, and he shall bless thy bread, and thy water; and I will take sickness away from the midst of thee.

Psalms 103:2-3 — Bless the LORD, O my soul, and forget not all his benefits: Who forgiveth all thine iniquities; who healeth all thy diseases.

Isaiah 53:4-5 — Surely he hath borne our griefs, and carried our sorrows: yet we did esteem him stricken, smitten of God, and afflicted. But he was wounded for our transgressions, he was bruised for our iniquities: the chastisement of our peace was upon him; and with his stripes we are healed.

Isaiah 58:8 — Then shall thy light break forth as the morning, and thine health shall spring forth speedily: and thy righteousness shall go before thee; the glory of the LORD shall be thy rereward(rear guard).

Matthew 8:17 — This was to fulfill what was spoken through Isaiah the prophet: "HE HIMSELF TOOK OUR INFIRMITIES AND CARRIED AWAY OUR DISEASES."

Romans 8:11 — But if the Spirit of Him who raised Jesus from the dead dwells in you, He who raised Christ Jesus from the dead will also give life to your mortal bodies through His Spirit who dwells in you.

I Peter 2:24 — ... and He Himself bore our sins in His body on the cross, so that we might die to sin and live to righteousness; for by His wounds you were healed.

4. Long Life

Deuteronomy 6:2 — That thou mightest fear the LORD thy God, to keep all his statutes and his commandments, which I command thee, thou, and thy son, and thy son's son, all the days of thy life; and that thy days may be prolonged.

Psalms 91:16	With long life will I satisfy him, and shew him my salvation.
Proverbs 9:11	For by me thy days shall be multiplied, and the years of thy life shall be increased.
Proverbs 10:27	The fear of the LORD prolongeth days: but the years of the wicked shall be shortened.
Ephesians 6:2-3	HONOR YOUR FATHER AND MOTHER (WHICH IS THE FIRST COMMANDMENT WITH A PROMISE.) SO THAT IT MAY BE WELL WITH YOU, AND THAT YOU MAY LIVE LONG ON THE EARTH.

5. Prosperity or Provision

Joshua 1:8	This book of the law shall not depart out of thy mouth; but thou shalt meditate therein day and night, that thou mayest observe to do according to all that is written therein: for then thou shalt make thy way prosperous, and then thou shalt have good success.
Psalms 23:1	The LORD is my shepherd; I shall not want. He maketh me to lie down in green pastures: he leadeth me beside the still waters.
Psalms 3:9-10	Honor the Lord with thy substance, and with the first fruits of all thine increase: so shall thy barns be filled with plenty, and thy presses shall burst out with new wine.
Proverbs 34:8-10	O taste and see that the LORD is good: blessed is the man that trusteth in him. O fear the LORD, ye his saints: for there is no want to them that fear him. The young lions do lack, and suffer hunger: but they that seek the LORD shall not want any good thing.

Malachi 3:10	Bring ye all the tithes into the storehouse, that there may be meat in mine house, and prove me now herewith, saith the LORD of hosts, if I will not open you the windows of heaven, and pour you out a blessing, that there shall not be room enough to receive it.
Philippians 4:19	And my God will supply all your needs according to His riches in glory in Christ Jesus.

6. Protection

Genesis 28:15	And, behold, I am with thee, and will keep thee in all places whither thou goest, and will bring thee again into this land; for I will not leave thee, until I have done that which I have spoken to thee of.
Psalms 91:1-4	He that dwelleth in the secret place of the most High shall abide under the shadow of the Almighty. I will say of the LORD, he is my refuge and my fortress: my God; in him will I trust. Surely he shall deliver thee from the snare of the fowler, and from the noisome pestilence. He shall cover thee with his feathers, and under his wings shalt thou trust: his truth shall be thy shield and buckler.
Psalms 91:10-11	There shall no evil befall thee, neither shall any plague come nigh thy dwelling. For he shall give his angels charge over thee, to keep thee in all thy ways.
Isaiah 54:17	No weapon that is formed against thee shall prosper; and every tongue that shall rise against thee in judgment thou shalt condemn. This is the heritage of the servants of the LORD, and their righteousness is of me, saith the LORD.
John 17:12	"While I was with them, I was keeping them in Your name which You have given Me; and I guarded them and not one of them perished but the son of perdition, so that the Scripture would be fulfilled."

II Thessalonians 3:3	But the Lord is faithful, and He will strengthen and protect you from the evil one.
Jude 24-25	Now to Him is able to keep you from stumbling, and to make you stand in the presence of His glory blameless with great joy, to the only God our Savior, through Jesus Christ our Lord, be glory, majesty, dominion and authority, before all time and now and forever. Amen.

7. Wisdom

Proverbs 4:5	Get wisdom, get understanding: forget it not; neither decline from the words of my mouth.
Proverbs 4:7	Wisdom is the principal thing; therefore get wisdom: and with all thy getting get understanding.
Proverbs 8:1	Doth not wisdom cry? and understanding put forth her voice?
Proverbs 13:10	Only by pride cometh contention: but with the well advised is wisdom.
Colossians 1: 9	For this reason also, since the day we heard of it, we have not ceased to pray for you and to ask that you may be filled with the knowledge of His will in all spiritual wisdom and understanding,
James 1:5	But if any of you lacks wisdom, let him ask of God, who gives to all generously and without reproach, and it will be given to him.

As you pray also use these scriptures

Psalms 68:19	Blessed be the Lord, who daily loadeth us with benefits, even the God of our salvation. Selah.
Isaiah 59:21	As for me, this is my covenant with them, saith the LORD; My spirit that is upon thee, and my words

	which I have put in thy mouth, shall not depart out of thy mouth, nor out of the mouth of thy seed, nor out of the mouth of thy seed's seed, saith the LORD, from henceforth and forever.
John 3:3	Jesus answered and said to him, "Truly, truly, I say to you, unless one is born again he cannot see the kingdom of God."
John 3:17	"For God did not send the Son into the world to judge the world, but that the world might be saved through Him."
Acts 4:12	"And there is salvation in no one else; for there is no other name under heaven that has been given among men by which we must be saved."
Romans 1:16	For I am not ashamed of the gospel, for it is the power of God for salvation to everyone who believes, to the Jew first and also to the Greek.
Romans 8:32	He who did not spare His own Son, but delivered Him over for us all, how will He not also with Him freely give us all things?
Romans 10:9-10	That if you confess with your mouth Jesus as Lord, and believe in your heart that God raised Him from the dead, you will be saved; for with the heart a person believes, resulting in righteousness, and with the mouth he confesses, resulting in salvation.
Romans 10:13	For "WHOEVER WILL CALL ON THE NAME OF THE LORD WILL BE SAVED."
Titus 2:11-12	For the grace of God has appeared, bringing salvation to all men, instructing us to deny ungodliness and worldly desires and to live sensibly, righteously and godly in the present age.

Hebrews 1:14   Are they not all ministering spirits, sent out to render service for the sake of those who will inherit salvation?

II Peter 3:9   The Lord is not slow about His promise, as some count slowness, but is patient toward you, not wishing for any to perish but for all to come to repentance.

Shield of Faith

Spiritual warfare is the biggest stumbling block to a Christian in receiving the blessings that God has for us. Satan is the one that puts all the doubts in our minds, telling us that we really don't deserve what we have asked God for. He continually tries to block our healings, our relationships, our finances, everything that we do. His biggest deception is in trying to tell us that we aren't worthy of salvation. He tries to tell us that we have to do a lot of things in order to get to heaven, when Jesus already did what was necessary.

Ephesians 6:10 tells us to draw our strength from the Lord and from His mighty power! We are to put on the armor of God to withstand the tactics of the devil.

THE ARMOR OF GOD

Ephesians 6:12-17   For our struggle is not against flesh and blood, but against the rulers, against the powers, against the world forces of this darkness, against the spiritual forces of wickedness in the heavenly places. Therefore, take up the full armor of God, so that you will be able to resist in the evil day, and having done everything, to stand firm. Stand firm therefore, HAVING GIRDED YOUR LOINS WITH TRUTH, and HAVING PUT ON THE BREASTPLATE OF RIGHTEOUSNESS, and having shod YOUR FEET WITH THE PREPARATION OF THE GOSPEL OF PEACE; in addition to all, taking up the shield of faith with which you will be able to extinguish all the flaming arrows of the evil one. And take THE HELMET OF SALVATION, and the sword of the Spirit, which is the word of God.

Use the following scriptures to help keep your faith strong.

Romans 8:11	But if the Spirit of Him who raised Jesus from the dead dwells in you, He who raised Christ Jesus from the dead will also give life to your mortal bodies through His Spirit who dwells in you.
Romans 10:17	So faith comes from hearing, and hearing by the word of Christ.
Romans 8:2	For the law of the Spirit of life in Christ Jesus has set you free from the law of sin and of death.
John 8:36	"So if the Son makes you free, you will be free indeed."
I John 4:4	You are from God, little children, and have overcome them; because greater is He who is in you than he who is in the world.
I John 3:8	"The one who practices sin is of the devil; for the devil has sinned from the beginning. The Son of God appeared for this purpose, to destroy the works of the devil."
John 14:13-14	Whatever you ask in My name, that will I do, so that the Father may be glorified in the Son. If you ask Me anything in My name, I will do it.
Colossians 1:19-20	For it was the Father's good pleasure for all the fullness to dwell in Him, and through Him to reconcile all things to Himself, having made peace through the blood of His cross; through Him, I say, whether things on earth or things in heaven.
II Corinthians 5:17	Therefore if anyone is in Christ, he is a new creature; the old things passed away; behold, new things have come.
I Corinthians 6:17	But the one who joins himself to the Lord is one spirit with Him.

I Corinthians 3:16	Do you not know that you are a temple of God and that the Spirit of God dwells in you?
Psalms 107:20	He sent his word, and healed them, and delivered them from their destructions.
Exodus 15:26	And said, If thou wilt diligently hearken to the voice of the LORD thy God, and wilt do that which is right in his sight, and wilt give ear to his commandments, and keep all his statutes, I will put none of these diseases upon thee, which I have brought upon the Egyptians: for I am the LORD that healeth thee.
I Peter 2:24	... and He Himself bore our sins in His body on the cross, so that we might die to sin and live to righteousness; for by His wounds you were healed.
Romans 8:32	He who did not spare His own Son, but delivered Him over for us all, how will He not also with Him freely give us all things?
Matthew 4:4	But He answered and said, "It is written," 'MAN SHALL NOT LIVE ON BREAD ALONE, BUT ON EVERY WORD THAT PROCEEDS OUT OF THE MOUTH OF GOD.'
Psalms 17: 3-4	My mouth has not transgressed as humans always do. As your lips have instructed me, I have kept the way of the law.
Revelation 12:11	"And they overcame him because of the blood of the Lamb and because of the word of their testimony, and they did not love their life even when faced with death."
II Corinthians 2:14	But thanks be to God, who always leads us in triumph in Christ, and manifests through us the sweet aroma of the knowledge of Him in every place.

Romans 8:37 — But in all these things we overwhelmingly conquer through Him who loved us.

II Corinthians 10:4-5 — For the weapons of our warfare are not of the flesh, but divinely powerful for the destruction of fortresses. We are destroying speculations and every lofty thing raised up against the knowledge of God, and we are taking every thought captive to the obedience of Christ.

Sin

When we acknowledge our sins and confess them to God, an amazing thing happens to them, as scripture shows us.

We are cleansed:

Psalms 51:7 — Purge me with hyssop, and I shall be clean: wash me, and I shall be whiter than snow.

Isaiah 1:18 — Come now, and let us reason together, saith the LORD: though your sins be as scarlet, they shall be as white as snow; though they be red like crimson, they shall be as wool.

We are forgiven:

Psalms 103:3-5 — Who forgiveth all thine iniquities; who healeth all thy diseases; Who redeemeth thy life from destruction; who crowneth thee with lovingkindness and tender mercies; Who satisfieth thy mouth with good things; so that thy youth is renewed like the eagle's.

Ephesians 1:7-9 — In Him we have redemption through His blood, the forgiveness of our trespasses, according to the riches of His grace which He lavished on us. In all wisdom and insight He made known to us the mystery of His will, according to His kind intention which He purposed in Him.

Colossians 2:13	When you were dead in your transgressions and the uncircumcision of your flesh, He made you alive together with Him, having forgiven us all our transgressions,
I John 1:9	If we confess our sins, He is faithful and righteous to forgive us our sins and to cleanse us from all unrighteousness.

They are removed from us:

Psalms 103:12	As far as the east is from the west, so far hath he removed our transgressions from us.
Isaiah 38:17	Behold, for peace I had great bitterness: but thou hast in love to my soul delivered it from the pit of corruption: for thou hast cast all my sins behind thy back.

He blots them out:

Isaiah 43:25	I, even I, am he that blotteth out thy transgressions for mine own sake, and will not remember thy sins.
Isaiah 44:22	I have blotted out, as a thick cloud, thy transgressions, and, as a cloud, thy sins: return unto me; for I have redeemed thee.

God lays our sins on Jesus:

Isaiah 53:6	All we like sheep have gone astray; we have turned every one to his own way; and the LORD hath laid on him the iniquity of us all.
John 3:16	"For God so loved the world, that He gave His only begotten Son, that whoever believes in Him shall not perish, but have eternal life."
I John 1:7	But if we walk in the Light as He Himself is in the Light, we have fellowship with one another, and the blood of Jesus His Son cleanses us from all sin.

God does not mention them again, nor remember them.

Ezekiel 18:22	All his transgressions that he hath committed, they shall not be mentioned unto him: in his righteousness that he hath done he shall live.
Ezekiel 33:16	None of his sins that he hath committed shall be mentioned unto him: he hath done that which is lawful and right; he shall surely live.
Hebrews 10:17	"AND THEIR SINS AND THEIR LAWLESS DEEDS I WILL REMEMBER NO MORE."
Romans 4:7-8	"BLESSED ARE THOSE WHOSE LAWLESS DEEDS HAVE BEEN FORGIVEN, AND WHOSE SINS HAVE BEEN COVERED. BLESSED IS THE MAN WHOSE SIN THE LORD WILL NOT TAKE INTO ACCOUNT."

Strength

Psalms 27:14	Wait on the LORD: be of good courage, and he shall strengthen thine heart: wait, I say, on the LORD.
Psalms 28:8	The LORD is their strength, and he is the saving strength of his anointed.
Psalms 29:11	The LORD will give strength unto his people; the LORD will bless his people with peace.
Psalms 46:1	God is our refuge and strength, a very present help in trouble.
Psalms 68:28	Thy God hath commanded thy strength: strengthen, O God, that which thou hast wrought for us.
Psalms 118:14	The LORD is my strength and song, and is become my salvation.

Psalms 138:3	In the day when I cried thou answeredst me, and strengthenedst me with strength in my soul.
Isaiah 30:15	For thus saith the Lord GOD, the Holy One of Israel; In returning and rest shall ye be saved; in quietness and in confidence shall be your strength: and ye would not.
Isaiah 40:29	He giveth power to the faint; and to them that have no might he increaseth strength.
Isaiah 40:31	But they that wait upon the LORD shall renew their strength; they shall mount up with wings as eagles; they shall run, and not be weary; and they shall walk, and not faint.
Isaiah 41:10	Fear thou not; for I am with thee: be not dismayed; for I am thy God: I will strengthen thee; yea, I will help thee; yea, I will uphold thee with the right hand of my righteousness.
Ephesians 3:16	That He would grant you, according to the riches of His glory, to be strengthened with power through His Spirit in the inner man.
Ephesians 6:10	Finally, be strong in the Lord and in the strength of His might.
I Peter 5:10	After you have suffered for a little while, the God of all grace, who called you to His eternal glory in Christ, will Himself perfect, confirm, strengthen and establish you.
Philippians 4:13	I can do all things through Him who strengthens me.

Temptation

I Corinthians 10:13	No temptation has overtaken you but such as is common to man; and God is faithful, who will not allow you to be tempted beyond what you are able,

	but with the temptation will provide the way of escape also, so that you will be able to endure it.
II Corinthians 11:3	But I am afraid that, as the serpent deceived Eve by his craftiness, your minds will be led astray from the simplicity and purity of devotion to Christ.
Hebrews 2:18	For since He Himself was tempted in that which He has suffered, He is able to come to the aid of those who are tempted.
Hebrews 4:15	For we do not have a high priest who cannot sympathize with our weaknesses, but One who has been tempted in all things as we are, yet without sin.
James 1:2-3	Consider it all joy, my brethren, when you encounter various trials, knowing that the testing of your faith produces endurance.
James 1:12	Blessed is a man who perseveres under trial; for once he has been approved, he will receive the crown of life which the Lord has promised to those who love Him.
II Peter 2:9	... then the Lord knows how to rescue the godly from temptation, and to keep the unrighteous under punishment for the day of judgment.

Tithing

Psalms 50: 14-15	Offer unto God thanksgiving; and pay thy vows unto the most High: And call upon me in the day of trouble: I will deliver thee, and thou shalt glorify me.
Proverbs 3:9-10	Honour the LORD with thy substance, and with the first fruits of all thine increase: So shall thy barns be filled with plenty, and thy presses shall burst out with new wine.
Proverbs 10:4	He becometh poor that dealeth with a slack hand: but the hand of the diligent maketh rich.

Proverbs 11: 24-25	There is that scattereth, and yet increaseth; and there is that withholdeth more than is meet, but it tendeth to poverty. The liberal soul shall be made fat: and he that watereth shall be watered also himself.
Proverbs 19:17	He that hath pity upon the poor lendeth unto the LORD; and that which he hath given will he pay him again.
Ecclesiastes 5:4	When thou vowest a vow unto God, defer not to pay it; for he hath no pleasure in fools: pay that which thou hast vowed.
Malachi 3:10	Bring ye all the tithes into the storehouse, that there may be meat in mine house, and prove me now herewith, saith the LORD of hosts, if I will not open you the windows of heaven, and pour you out a blessing, that there shall not be room enough to receive it.
Matthew 25:40	The King will answer and say to them, 'Truly I say to you, to the extent that you did it to one of these brothers of Mine, even the least of them, you did it to Me."
Luke 6:38	"Give, and it will be given to you. They will pour into your lap a good measure—pressed down, shaken together, and running over. For by your standard of measure it will be measured to you in return."
Romans 12:13	... contributing to the needs of the saints, practicing hospitality.

Tribulation

Psalms 119:71	It is good for me that I have been afflicted; that I might learn thy statutes.
Romans 5:3-5	And not only this, but exult in our tribulations, knowing that tribulation brings about perseverance;

	and perseverance, proven character; and proven character, hope; and hope does not disappoint, because the love of God has been poured out within our hearts through the Holy Spirit who was given to us.
Romans 8:18	For I consider that the sufferings of this present time are not worthy to be compared with the glory that is to be revealed to us.
Romans 8:35	Who will separate us from the love of Christ? Will tribulation, or distress, or persecution, or famine, or nakedness, or peril, or sword?
II Corinthians 1:3-4	Blessed be the God and Father of our Lord Jesus Christ, the Father of mercies and God of all comfort, who comforts us in all our affliction so that we will be able to comfort those who are in any affliction with the comfort with which we ourselves are comforted by God.
II Corinthians 1:7	... and our hope for you is firmly grounded, knowing that as you are sharers of our sufferings, so also you are sharers of our comfort.

Trust

Trust your unknown future to our all-knowing God.

Psalms 20:6-7	Now know that I the LORD saveth his anointed; he will hear him from his holy heaven with the saving strength of his right hand. Some trust in chariots, and some in horses: but we will remember the name of the LORD our God.
Psalms 25: 1-2	Unto thee, O LORD, do I lift up my soul. O my God, I trust in thee: let me not be ashamed, let not mine enemies triumph over me.
Psalms 40:5	Many, O LORD my God, are thy wonderful works

	which thou hast done, and thy thoughts which are to us-ward: they cannot be reckoned up in order unto thee: if I would declare and speak of them, they are more than can be numbered.
Psalms 115:11	Ye that fear the LORD, trust in the LORD: he is their help and their shield.
Psalms 119:42	So shall I have wherewith to answer him that reproacheth me: for I trust in thy word.
Proverbs 3:5-6	Trust in the LORD with all thine heart; and lean not unto thine own understanding. In all thy ways acknowledge him, and he shall direct thy paths.
Isaiah 12:2	Behold, God is my salvation; I will trust, and not be afraid: for the LORD JEHOVAH is my strength and my song; he also is become my salvation.
Isaiah 26:4	Trust ye in the LORD forever: for in the LORD JEHOVAH is everlasting strength:
1 Thessalonians 2:4	... but just as we have been approved by God to be entrusted with the gospel, so we speak, not as pleasing men, but God who examines our hearts.

Voices-Testing

Psalms 1:1	Blessed is the man that walketh not in the counsel of the ungodly, nor standeth in the way of sinners, nor sitteth in the seat of the scornful.

The ungodly has a voice which leads the sinner. This is their own spirit, the spirit of flesh or the spirit of the devil.

Romans 8:15	For you have not received a spirit of slavery leading to fear again, but you have received a spirit of adoption as sons by which we cry out, "Abba! Father!"
II Timothy 1:7	For God has not given us a spirit of timidity, but of

	power and love and discipline. **Only the evil spirit causes fear.**
Psalms 1:1	Blessed is the man that walketh not in the counsel of the ungodly, nor standeth in the way of sinners, nor sitteth in the seat of the scornful. The ungodly has a voice which leads the sinner. This is their own spirit, the spirit of flesh or the spirit of the devil.
Romans 8:15	For you have not received a spirit of slavery leading to fear again, but you have received a spirit of adoption as sons by which we cry out, "Abba! Father!"
II Timothy 1:7	For God has not given us a spirit of timidity, but of power and love and discipline.

Every voice has meaning!

1 Corinthians 14:11	If then I do not know the meaning of the language, I will be to the one who speaks a barbarian, and the one who speaks will be a barbarian to me.

You need to seek agreement in God's word. He won't change the scriptures to fit the voice of the evil one, and when He gives you guidance and direction He won't nullify His own word.

Hebrews 8:10	"FOR THIS IS THE COVENANT THAT I WILL MAKE WITH THE HOUSE OF ISRAEL AFTER THOSE DAYS, SAYS THE LORD: I WILL PUT MY LAWS INTO THEIR MINDS, AND I WILL WRITE THEM ON THEIR HEARTS. AND I WILL BE THEIR GOD AND THEY SHALL BE MY PEOPLE."
I John 2:20	But you have an anointing from the Holy One, and you all know.
I John 2:27	As for you, the anointing which you received from

Him abides in you, and you have no need for anyone to teach you; but as His anointing teaches you about all things, and is true and is not a lie, and just as it has taught you, you abide in Him.

John 10:3 "To him the doorkeeper opens, and the sheep hear his voice, and he calls his own sheep by name and leads them out."

John 10:27 "My sheep hear My voice, and I know them, and they follow Me."

Use these scriptures to help you know the difference between the voice of Jesus and the voice of someone trying to deceive you. In addition to John 10:3,27 use:

John 18:37 Therefore Pilate said to Him, "So You are a king?" Jesus answered, "You say correctly that I am a king. For this I have been born, and for this I have come into the world, to testify to the truth. Everyone who is of the truth hears My voice."

I Corinthians 12:3 Therefore I make known to you that no one speaking by the Spirit of God says, "Jesus is accursed;" and no one can say, "Jesus is Lord," except by the Holy Spirit.

When the Lord speaks to us:

I Corinthians 2:13 Which things we also speak, not in words taught by human wisdom, but in those taught by the Spirit, combining spiritual thoughts with spiritual words.

You will know by His Spirit inside of you that Jesus is speaking to you, even though He uses words that aren't familiar to you.

John 14: 27 "Peace I leave with you; My peace I give to you; not as the world gives do I give to you. Do not let your heart be troubled, nor let it be fearful."

You will have peace inwardly when it is Jesus who is speaking.

Proverbs 3:5-6   Trust in the LORD with all thine heart; and lean not unto thine own understanding. In all thy ways acknowledge him, and he shall direct thy paths.

You will know, that you know, when you trust in Jesus.

Isaiah 30:15   For thus saith the Lord GOD, the Holy One of Israel; In returning and rest shall ye be saved; in quietness and in confidence shall be your strength and ye would not.

You will have confidence and assurance.

II Peter 1:19   So we have the prophetic word made more sure, to which you do well to pay attention as to a lamp shining in a dark place, until the day dawns and the morning star arises in your hearts.

I Thess. 5:19-21   Do not quench the Spirit; do not despise prophetic utterances. But examine everything carefully; hold fast to that which is good.

Psalms 119:89   Forever, O LORD, thy word is settled in heaven.

God will not change His Word for anyone's convenience. You must check any messages with the Bible to see if they are from Jesus or some other place.

II Corinthians 13:1   This is the third time I am coming to you. EVERY FACT IS TO BE CONFIRMED BY THE TESTIMONY OF TWO OR THREE WITNESSES.

God always confirms His Word to you through scripture.

II Corinthians 4:4   In whose case the god of this world has blinded the minds of the unbelieving so that they might not see the light of the gospel of the glory of Christ, who is the image of God.

Joseph and Ruth Wesley ❧ 163

I Corinthians 12:3   Therefore I make known to you that no one speaking by the Spirit of God says, "Jesus is accursed"; and no one can say, "Jesus is Lord," except by the Holy Spirit.

Satan will not call Jesus "LORD" even though he may use the word 'god' when he tries to deceive someone.

II Corinthians 1:20   For as many as are the promises of God, in Him they are yes; therefore also through Him is our Amen to the glory of God through us.

Jesus always speaks clearly and you will have no doubt that it is He that is speaking.

When the Devil speaks:

Romans 8:1   Therefore there is now no condemnation for those who are in Christ Jesus.

I John 3:19-20   We will know by this that we are of the truth, and will assure our heart before Him in whatever our heart condemns us; for God is greater than our heart and knows all things.

Revelation 12:10   Then I heard a loud voice in heaven, saying, "Now the salvation, and the power, and the kingdom of our God and the authority of His Christ have come, for the accuser of our brethren has been thrown down, he who accuses them before our God day and night."

Satan will try to accuse us of the sins that we have already confessed and make us feel guilty about them.

I John 4:1-6   Beloved, do not believe every spirit, but test the spirits to see whether they are from God, because many false prophets have gone out into the world. By this you know the Spirit of God: every spirit that confesses that Jesus Christ has come in the flesh is from God; and every spirit that does not confess Jesus is not from God; this is the spirit of the antichrist, of which you have heard that it is coming, and now it is already in the world. You are from God, little children, and have overcome them; because greater is He who is in you than he who is in the world. They are from the world; therefore they speak as from the world, and the world listens to them. We are from God; he who knows God listens to us; he who is not from God does not listen to us. By this we know the spirit of truth and the spirit of error.

Satan tries to tell us that Jesus is not Lord. This is another one of his deceptions.

James 3:16   For where jealousy and selfish ambition exist, there is disorder and every evil thing.

If you are confused and have to "work it out" then it is not from God. Satan is the author of confusion.

Hebrews 4:12   For the word of God is living and active and sharper than any two-edged sword, and piercing as far as the division of soul and spirit, of both joints and marrow, and able to judge the thoughts and intentions of the heart.

II Timothy 1:7   For God has not given us a spirit of timidity, but of power and love and discipline.

Romans 8:15   For you have not received a spirit of slavery leading to fear again, but you have received a spirit of adoption as sons by which we cry out, "Abba! Father!"

Satan tries to create doubt and fear in us when we pray and tells us that we don't really know what to pray for. He tries to tell us the opposite of what God says and take away God's word. He often says to us, "What if it doesn't work?" when we try to do something.

When our own flesh gets in the way

Romans 8: 5-7   For those who are according to the flesh set their minds on the things of the flesh, but those who are according to the Spirit, the things of the Spirit. For the mind set on the flesh is death, but the mind set on the Spirit is life and peace, because the mind set on the flesh is hostile toward God; for it does not subject itself to the law of God, for it is not even able to do so.

Our flesh has to think before it speaks, while God's Word just flows.

Hebrews 5:12   For though by this time you ought to be teachers, you have need again for someone to teach you the elementary principles of the oracles of God, and you have come to need milk and not solid food.

We need God's Word constantly before us so we become mature in Christ.

James 1:7-8   For that man not ought to think that he will receive anything from the Lord, *being* a double-minded man, unstable in all his ways..

Do not be double minded.

John 14:16   "I will ask the Father, and He will give you another Helper, that He may be with you forever."

John 16:13   But when He, the Spirit of truth, comes, He will guide you into all the truth; for He will not speak on His own initiative, but whatever He hears, He will speak; and He will disclose to you what is to come.

This helps us to be stable because Satan wants us to be confused about our decisions.

Visions

Numbers 12:6-8   And he said, Hear now my words: If there be a prophet among you, I the LORD will make myself known unto him in a vision, and will speak unto him in a dream. My servant Moses is not so, who is faithful in all mine house. With him will I speak mouth to mouth, even apparently, and not in dark speeches; and the similitude of the LORD shall he behold: wherefore then were ye not afraid to speak against my servant Moses?

Joel 2:28-29 And it shall come to pass afterward, that I will pour out my spirit upon all flesh; and your sons and your daughters shall prophesy, your old men shall dream dreams, your young men shall see visions: And also upon the servants and upon the handmaids in those days will I pour out my spirit.

Acts 2:17-18 'AND IT SHALL BE IN THE LAST DAYS,' God says, 'THAT I WILL POUR FORTH OF MY SPIRIT ON ALL MANKIND; AND YOUR SONS AND YOUR DAUGHTERS SHALL PROPHESY, AND YOUR YOUNG MEN SHALL SEE VISIONS, AND YOUR OLD MEN SHALL DREAM DREAMS; EVEN ON MY BOND-SLAVES, BOTH MEN AND WOMEN, I WILL IN THOSE DAYS POUR FORTH OF MY SPIRIT' And they shall prophesy.

Weight Control

Dieting is one of the most talked about things in our society today. Many of us are under a bondage because we are either thinking about what and how much we have eaten, or planning on what we should, and feeling guilty because it wasn't the right thing. Many of us are under condemnation from this.

This is Satan's big deception to us. He knows that our bodies are the temples of the Holy Spirit, and he would like to tempt us to give in to the desires to eat those things that are unhealthy for us. Satan would like us to turn to food for comfort or to help us feel good. At times He makes these desires so overwhelming, that we feel helpless or powerless to do anything about them. If at times we are tired, sick, lonely, angry or emotionally attacked by the enemy, then we need to call out to God to help us come against the desire to eat in order to satisfy those feelings.

It is always good to have someone to be your prayer partner while you are trying to control your weight. Not to make you feel guilty or under further condemnation, but to really pray for you as you are coming against the enemy.

First bind Satan out loud in the name of Jesus, and ask for an infilling of the Holy Spirit.

Matthew 18:18 says, " Amen, I say to you, whatever you bind on earth shall be bound in Heaven; and whatever you loose on earth shall be loosed in heaven."

Remember to take one day at a time and thank God for helping you to overcome Satan. The following scriptures can help.

Psalms 27:11	Teach me thy way, O LORD, and lead me in a plain path, because of mine enemies.
Proverbs 25:16	Hast thou found honey? Eat so much as is sufficient for thee, lest thou be filled therewith, and vomit it.
Matthew 6:25	"For this reason I say to you, do not be worried about your life, as to what you will eat or what you will drink; nor for your body, as to what you will put on. Is not life more than food, and the body more than clothing?"
Mark 8:34	And He summoned the crowd with His disciples, and said to them, "If anyone wishes to come after Me, he must deny himself, and take up his cross and follow Me."
Acts 20:28	"Be on guard for yourselves and for all the flock, among which the Holy Spirit has made you overseers, to shepherd the church of God which He purchased with His own blood."
Romans 8:13-14	... for if you are living according to the flesh, you must die; but if by the Spirit you are putting to death the deeds of the body, you will live. For all who are being led by the Spirit of God, these are sons of God.

Romans 14:2-3	One person has faith that he may eat all things, but he who is weak eats vegetables only. The one who eats is not to regard with contempt the one who does not eat, and the one who does not eat is not to judge the one who eats, for God has accepted him.
Romans 14:17	... for the kingdom of God is not eating and drinking, but righteousness and peace and joy in the Holy Spirit.
I Corinthians 6:12	All things are lawful for me, but not all things are profitable. All things are lawful for me, but I will not be mastered by anything.
I Corinthians 9:25	Everyone who competes in the games exercises self-control in all things. They then do it to receive a perishable wreath, but we an imperishable.
I Corinthians 10:31	Whether, then, you eat or drink or whatever you do, do all to the glory of God.
II Corinthians 1:3-4	Blessed be the God, and Father of our Lord Jesus Christ, the Father of mercies and God of all comfort, who comforts us in all our affliction so that we will be able to comfort those who are in any affliction with the comfort with which we ourselves are comforted by God.
Galatians 5:13	For you were called to freedom, brethren; only do not turn your freedom into an opportunity for the flesh, but through love serve one another.
Ephesians 1:4-7	Just as He chose us in Him before the foundation of the world, that we would be holy and blameless before Him. In love He predestined us to adoption as sons through Jesus Christ to Himself, according to the kind intention of His will, to the praise of the glory of His grace, which He freely bestowed on us in the Beloved. In Him we have redemption through His blood, the forgiveness of our trespasses, according to the riches of His grace.

Titus 2:11-12	For the grace of God has appeared, bringing salvation to all men, instructing us to deny ungodliness and worldly desires and to live sensibly, righteously and godly in the present age,
Hebrews 4:16	Therefore let us draw near with confidence to the throne of grace, so that we may receive mercy and find grace to help in time of need.
Hebrews 10:35-36	Therefore, do not throw away your confidence, which has a great reward. For you have need of endurance, so that when you have done the will of God, you may receive what was promised.

Will of God

I John 5:14-15	This is the confidence which we have before Him, that, if we ask anything according to His will, He hears us. And if we know that He hears us in whatever we ask, we know that we have the requests which we have asked from Him.
John 15: 7	"If you abide in Me, and My words abide in you, ask whatever you wish, and it will be done for you."
John 7:17	"If anyone is willing to do His will, he will know of the teaching, whether it is of God or whether I speak from Myself."
Matthew 6:10	'Your kingdom come, Your will be done, On earth as it is in heaven.'
Matthew 18:19-20	"Again I say to you, that if two of you agree on earth about anything that they may ask, it shall be done for them by My Father who is in heaven. For where two or three have gathered together in My name, I am there in their midst."

Matthew 25:40	The King will answer and say to them, "Truly I say to you, to the extent that you did it to one of these brothers of Mine, even the least of them, you did it to Me."
Matthew 22:37-38	And He said to him, "YOU SHALL LOVE THE LORD YOUR GOD WITH ALL YOUR HEART, AND WITH ALL YOUR SOUL, AND WITH ALL YOUR MIND." This is the great and foremost commandment.
Matthew 28:19-20	"Go therefore and make disciples of all the nations, baptizing them in the name of the Father and the Son and the Holy Spirit, teaching them to observe all that I commanded you; and lo, I am with you always, even to the end of the age."
Mark 16:15	And He said to them, "Go into all the world and preach the gospel to all creation."
Romans 8:27	... and He who searches the hearts knows what the mind of the Spirit is, because He intercedes for the saints according to the will of God.
Romans 12:2	And do not be conformed to this world, but be transformed by the renewing of your mind, so that you may prove what the will of God is, that which is good and acceptable and perfect.
Philippians 2:13	... for it is God who is at work in you, both to will and to work for His good pleasure.
I Thess. 5:16-18	Rejoice always; pray without ceasing; in everything give thanks; for this is God's will for you in Christ Jesus.

Wisdom

Psalms 25:4-5	Shew me thy ways, O LORD; teach me thy paths. Lead me in thy truth, and teach me: for thou art the God of my salvation; on thee do I wait all the day.

Psalms 119:130	The entrance of thy words giveth light; it giveth understanding unto the simple.
Psalms 119:135	Make thy face to shine upon thy servant; and teach me thy statutes.
Proverbs 2:6-7	For the LORD giveth wisdom: out of his mouth cometh knowledge and understanding. He layeth up sound wisdom for the righteous: he is a buckler to them that walk uprightly.
Proverbs 9:10	The fear of the LORD is the beginning of wisdom: and the knowledge of the Holy One is understanding.
John 14:26	"But the Helper, the Holy Spirit, whom the Father will send in My name, He will teach you all things, and bring to your remembrance all that I said to you."
I Corinthians 1:30	But by His doing you are in Christ Jesus, who became to us wisdom from God, and righteousness and sanctification, and redemption,
Ephesians 1:17	That the God of our Lord Jesus Christ, the Father of glory, may give to you a spirit of wisdom and of revelation in the knowledge of Him.
Colossians 1:9	For this reason also, since the day we heard of it, we have not ceased to pray for you and to ask that you may be filled with the knowledge of His will in all spiritual wisdom and understanding,
Colossians 1:28	We proclaim Him, admonishing every man and teaching every man with all wisdom, so that we may present every man complete in Christ.
James 1:5	But if any of you lacks wisdom, let him ask of God, who gives to all generously and without reproach, and it will be given to him.

James 3:17	But the wisdom from above is first pure, then peaceable, gentle, reasonable, full of mercy and good fruits, unwavering, without hypocrisy.

Word

Numbers 23:19	God is not a man, that he should lie; neither the son of man, that he should repent: hath he said, and shall he not do it ? or hath he spoken, and shall he not make it good?
Deuteronomy 30:14	But the word is very nigh unto thee, in thy mouth, and in thy heart, that thou mayest do it.
Psalms 107:20	He sent his word, and healed them, and delivered them from their destructions.
Psalms 119:89	For ever, O LORD, thy word is settled in heaven.
Psalms 119:105	Thy word is a lamp unto my feet, and a light unto my path.
Psalms 119:107	I am afflicted very much: quicken me, O LORD, according unto thy word.
Psalms 119:130	The entrance of thy words giveth light; it giveth understanding unto the simple.
Psalms 119:133	Order my steps in thy word: and let not any iniquity have dominion over me.
Proverbs 18:21	Death and life are in the power of the tongue: and they that love it shall eat the fruit thereof.
Proverbs 30:5-6	Every word of God is pure: he is a shield unto them that put their trust in him. Add thou not unto his words, lest he reprove thee, and thou be found a liar.
Isaiah 40:8	The grass withereth, the flower fadeth: but the word of our God shall stand for ever.

Matthew 4:4	But He answered and said, "It is written, 'MAN SHALL NOT LIVE ON BREAD ALONE, BUT ON EVERY WORD THAT PROCEEDS OUT OF THE MOUTH OF GOD.' "
Matthew 24:35	"Heaven and earth will pass away, but my words will not pass away."
John 1:1	In the beginning was the Word, and the Word was with God, and the Word was God.
John 1:14	And the Word became flesh, and dwelt among us, and we saw His glory, glory as of the only begotten from the Father, full of grace and truth.
John 15:7	"If you abide in Me, and My words abide in you, ask whatever you wish, and it will be done for you."
John 17:17	"Sanctify them in the truth; Your word is truth."
Romans 10:8	But what does it say? "THE WORD IS NEAR YOU, IN YOUR MOUTH AND IN YOUR HEART"—that is, the word of faith which we are preaching,
Romans 10:17	So faith comes from hearing, and hearing by the word of Christ.
Hebrews 1:1-3	God, after He spoke long ago to the fathers in the prophets in many portions and in many ways, in these last days has spoken to us in His Son, whom He appointed heir of all things, through whom also He made the world. And He is the radiance of His glory and the exact representation of His nature, and upholds all things by the word of His power. When He had made purification of sins, He sat down at the right hand of the Majesty on high,

Hebrews 4:12	For the word of God is living and active and sharper than any two-edged sword, and piercing as far as the division of soul and spirit, of both joints and marrow, and able to judge the thoughts and intentions of the heart.
II Thessalonians 3:1	Finally brethren, pray for us that the word of the Lord will spread rapidly and be glorified, just as it did also with you.
I Peter 1:23	For you have been born again not of seed which is perishable but imperishable, that is, through the living and enduring word of God.
I Peter 1:25	"BUT THE WORD OF THE LORD ENDURES FOREVER." And this is the word which was preached to you.
I John 2:14	I have written to you, fathers, because you know Him who has been from the beginning. I have written to you, young men, because you are strong, and the word of God abides in you, and you have overcome the evil one.
Revelation 12:11	"And they overcame him because of the blood of the Lamb and because of the word of their testimony, and they did not love their life even when faced with death."

Date	Request–Details	God's Promises	Answer & Date

Date	Request–Details	God's Promises	Answer & Date

Prayer Team
Telephone # and Address

Name	Address	Phone Number	Email

Praying God's Promises Praying God's Promises Praying God's Promises Praying God's Promises Praying God's Promises Praying God's Promises Praying God's Promises

Pass the blessing on...

"*Praying God's Promises*"
*If you know of a book store, church or reseller
who will appreciate this book; have them contact:*

<u>www.publisher@rivercitypress.net</u>

RIVER CITY PRESS
Publishing "Life-changing Books"
4301 Emerson Avenue North
Minneapolis, MN 55412
612-521-9633